Emerging Dynamics in Contemporary India–Malaysia Relations

MODERN SOUTHEAST ASIA

Series Editor:

Sunil Kukreja, University of Puget Sound

Advisory Board:

Amy L. Freedman, Rachel Harrison, Ravichandran Moorthy, and Farish A. Noor

The increased visibility and prominence of Southeast Asia and the societies therein on the global stage during the early years of the 21st century have attracted a deservedly rich and vibrant interest among academics, policy-makers, and social commentators. Southeast Asia collectively constitutes one of the most diverse, dynamic, and globally critical regions. This series provides a compelling platform for a diverse range of scholars to engage in discourses on the multitude of critical and timely intra-regional, trans-regional, and societal-specific analyses pertaining to Southeast Asia. The series welcomes proposals and manuscripts from the various social sciences and humanities, including contributions that profile interdisciplinary scholarship which makes a distinctive contribution to the understanding of Southeast Asia.

Titles in the Series

Emerging Dynamics in Contemporary India–Malaysia Relations

Edited by Ravichandran Moorthy and Sarjit S. Gill

LEXINGTON BOOKS
Lanham • Boulder • New York • London

Rowman & Littlefield
Bloomsbury Publishing Inc, 1359 Broadway, New York, NY 10018, USA
Bloomsbury Publishing Plc, 50 Bedford Square, London, WC1B 3DP, UK
Bloomsbury Publishing Ireland, 29 Earlsfort Terrace, Dublin 2, D02 AY28, Ireland
www.bloomsbury.com

Published by Lexington Books
An imprint of The Rowman & Littlefield Publishing Group, Inc.
4501 Forbes Boulevard, Suite 200, Lanham, Maryland 20706
www.rowman.com
86-90 Paul Street, London EC2A 4NE

British Library Cataloguing in Publication Information available

Library of Congress Cataloging-in-Publication Data

Names: Gill, Sarjit S., editor. | Moorthy, Ravichandran, editor.
Title: Emerging dynamics in contemporary India-Malaysia relations / edited by Sarjit S.
    Gill and Ravichandran Moorthy.
Description: Lanham : Lexington Books, [2023] | Series: Modern Southeast Asia |
    Includes bibliographical references and index.
Identifiers: LCCN 2023003002 (print) | LCCN 2023003003 (ebook) |
    ISBN 9781666936988 (cloth) | ISBN 9781666936995 (ebook)
Subjects: LCSH: India–Relations–Malaysia. | Malaysia–Relations–India. | India–
    Social conditions–21st century. | Malaysia–Social conditions–21st century. | India–
    Economic conditions–21st century. | Malaysia–Economic conditions–21st century.
Classification: LCC DS450.M4 E44 2023 (print) | LCC DS450.M4 (ebook) | DDC
    327.540595–dc23/eng/20230124
LC record available at https://lccn.loc.gov/2023003002
LC ebook record available at https://lccn.loc.gov/2023003003

Contents

Introduction

Contemporary India–
Malaysia Relations

Ravichandran Moorthy and Sarjit S. Gill

Malaysia and India had shared ethnoreligious and socio-cultural bonds through trade, conquest, and migration for centuries. Prior to the arrival of Islam in the early fifteenth century, Hindu-Buddhist traditions dominated the Malay world through government structures, ideas and philosophy, religious pursuits, and civilizational influences. Many of the local practices and languages have been greatly influenced by these traditions—evident till today in many societies in the archipelago and mainland Southeast Asia. Indian merchant ships have traversed the seas of the Malay Archipelago, conducting trade in the numerous ports in the region. Along with trade, the Indians brought their culture, practices and religions, which were later embraced by the people and governments of the region. Indians refer to the Malay Peninsula as *Suvarnadvipa*—the golden island or peninsula (which may have included the regions of Borneo, Sumatera and Java) or *Suvarnabhumi*—the land of gold, as depicted in the classical Hindu text *Ramayana*. Archaeological evidence confirms the existence of several Indianized or partially Indianized settlements scattered along the northern section of the Malay Peninsula's west coast, such as Takola, Langkasuka, and Kadaram (Kedah). According to Chinese records, Langkasuka was the first Indianized kingdom in the peninsula in the second century B.C. (Winstedt, 1935). Archaeological evidence also suggested the existence of Indianized settlements in the states of Kedah and Perak (Wheatley, 1961). The Hindu chandis and Buddhist stupas found in the Bujang Valley, Kedah, proved that early Indians, in addition to trade, have started living in these areas and subsequently built religious structures for their worship needs. Kadaram (or Kedah) thrived politically and commercially under the rule of Sri Vijaya (Malay-Buddhist empire on the island of Sumatra) from the sixth to the seventh century. Even during the Islamic

1

period of Peninsula Malaya, Indian influence in trade, socio-culture, and governance structure was still widespread. During the Western colonial period, as early as 1511, Indian traders still played pivotal roles in making Southeast Asian ports flourish (Moorthy, 2016; Moorthy and Ummadevi, 2012).

India established diplomatic relations with the Federation of Malaya shortly after Malaya's independence in 1957. Malaya was later known as Malaysia after its merger with Singapore, Sabah and Sarawak in 1963. The two countries enjoyed a strong relationship in the 1960s due to the personal friendship between Prime Ministers Nehru and Tunku Abdul Rahman Putra. The spirit of the freedom movement against colonialism and oppression brought these leaders closer together in their quest to address postcolonial and Cold War dynamics. In 1957, India was one of the first countries to recognize Malaya's and later Malaysia's statehood and establish diplomatic relations. The 1960s were a turbulent period for India and Malaysia, with both countries embroiled in regional geopolitical conflicts with their immediate neighbours. Despite the difficulties, both countries maintained good relations, demonstrating outstanding statesmanship. During the Sino-Indian War of 1962, for example, Malaysia expressed sympathy for and stood by India, promising complete support. Tunku went on to launch the "Save Democracy Fund" crowdfunding campaign to help India fight Chinese aggression. During the war, Malaysia was the first Asian country to provide India with more than just moral support. Malaysia proved to be a reliable ally in times of crisis for India.

Between 1963 and 1966, President Sukarno of Indonesia launched a military offensive called *Ganyang Malaysia* against Malaysia. He was unhappy with the formation of the Federation of Malaysia, with Singapore, Sabah and Sarawak, which he saw as an attempt by the British to maintain colonial rule under the guise of independence. In this crisis, India supported the Federation of Malaysia and helped bring the issue into the international spotlight. For example, despite Sukarno's vehement opposition, India insisted on including Malaysia in the Second Afro-Asian Conference. In addition, Lal Bahadur Shastri, the then Indian Prime Minister, advocated for Malaysia's nonpermanent membership in the United Nations Security Council. In response, Indonesia pulled out of the United Nations in 1965. Malaysia also severed diplomatic ties with Pakistan in 1965 to show solidarity with India following the India-Pakistan war over Kashmir. This audacious move demonstrated that Malaysia values international ties more than religious ties (Bala Kishnan, 2020).

After Tunku Abdul Rahman, subsequent Malaysian prime ministers were also keen to develop a closer relationship with India in many facets of engagements, bilaterally and regionally, through ASEAN (Association of Southeast Asian Nations) initiatives and internationally. Over the years, India and Malaysia have developed close political, defence, economic, and socio-cultural ties, aided by a sizable ethnic Indian diaspora in Malaysia. However, relations with India during these periods had their fair share of issues, especially as Malaysia began to become more Islamic in its foreign policy outlook. Nevertheless, Malaysia's economic rise in the 1980s saw India becoming its reliable trading partner. India's relatively benign geo-politics towards Southeast Asia and having a vibrant Indian diaspora community in Malaysia facilitated relations between the two countries. When Najib Razak became Malaysia's sixth prime minister in April 2009, relations between the two countries started to endear more intensely. Najib's government took serious initiatives to strengthen relations with India. In January 2010, Najib held an inaugural official visit to India, and this was reciprocated by the Indian premier Manmohan Singh in October of the same year. During this visit, both countries agreed to collaborate on a Framework for Strategic Partnership, which envisions the development of a multifaceted relationship to elevate bilateral relations to the level of a long-term, strategic partnership.

During this visit, several MOUs were signed on Comprehensive Economic Cooperation (CECA), traditional systems of Indian medicine, tourism, innovation and R&D. Both Prime Ministers also inaugurated the "Little India" cultural project in Brickfields, Kuala Lumpur. There have been regular Summit level exchanges and meetings between ministers and senior officials in a variety of areas of mutual interest, including diplomatic, economic, and defence issues. Najib also attended the ASEAN-India Commemorative Summit in December 2012 in New Delhi, where he had a bilateral meeting with Manmohan Singh on a range of bilateral issues. Regarding trade, Malaysia is India's third-largest trading partner in ASEAN. Bilateral trade between Malaysia and India stood at US$12.8 billion in 2015–16, as against US$ 16.9 billion in 2014–15. The trade balance favours Malaysia (US$5.4 billion in 2015–16). The Prime Ministers have expressed their aspiration to see this trade increase to US$15 billion in the immediate future. In terms of investment, there has been significant growth between the two nations in various sectors. The total investments from Malaysia stood at around US$7 billion or more against total investments of around US$2.5 billion from the Indian side (MEA, 2017). Najib's India engagement is inextricably linked to Indians in Malaysia. During his visit, Najib acknowledged Malaysian Indians' pivotal role in bringing Malaysia and India closer together, saying they "constitute a special reason why it is so natural for our two countries to forge even closer and friendlier relations." Since the majority of Indians in Malaysia are from southern India and speak Tamil, Najib made an extra effort to connect with the state of Tamil Nadu in South India and the *Kollywood* (Tamil media industry), which has a strong influence among Indians in Malaysia (Izzuddin, 2017).

In May 2018, Malaysia experienced a significant political shift when Malaysians overwhelmingly decided to overthrow the ruling party, *Barisan Nasional* (B.N.), through the electoral process. The so-called "Malaysian tsunami" dethroned the political coalition that had been in power since 1957. Dr. Mahathir Mohamad, Malaysia's patriarch and fourth prime minister, was re-elected as the country's seventh prime minister in the May 2018 general election. Prime Minister Narendra Modi was among the first heads of state who met Mahathir in a brief stopover in Kuala Lumpur to congratulate him on his general election success personally and for being appointed Prime Minister. Modi also met Deputy Prime Minister Wan Azizah Wan Ismail and her husband Anwar Ibrahim. According to Malaysia's Foreign Ministry, the meeting between the leaders underscored the fundamental strength of the millennia-old relations between Malaysia and India. It demonstrated the strong commitment to strengthening their strategic partnership further. Both countries share centuries-old cultural and historical ties and collaboration in various fields, including infrastructure development, education, tourism, and defence. With total trade of RM61.43 billion (US$20.6 billion) in 2017, India is Malaysia's largest trading partner in South Asia (NST, June 1, 2018). However, despite initial goodwill gestures from both leaders, relations soured when Mahathir took an anti-India stance on the rise of Hindu nationalism, mishandling the Kashmir issue, and the Indian Citizenship Amendment Act (CAA). Things worsened when Mahathir refused to extradite fugitive Islamic Indian evangelist Zakir Naik to India, claiming that he would not receive justice in India. India reacted by privately urging Indian palm oil importers to boycott palm oil from Malaysia. However, bilateral relations appeared to slowly improve after Mahathir stepped down as Prime Minister in March 2020. Nevertheless, the resumption of previous warmth in India–Malaysia relations largely depends on the new government's ability to maintain neutrality in India–Pakistan disputes (Kachiar, 2020).

The main goal of this book is to capture the many facets of Malaysia–India bilateral relations, both conceptually and empirically. In addition to the Introduction, this book is divided into six chapters. In Chapter 1, Malaysia–India Bilateral Relations: History, Issues, Challenges, and Prospects, the authors present the historical narrative of Malaysia–India bilateral relations from the British colonial period to Mahathir's second premiership. Relations between these countries had existed for several centuries before the arrival of Portuguese traders to Southeast Asia. In effect, until 1511 A.D., there was an era of Malayan history known as the "Indian age." However, beginning with the British colonial period in the nineteenth century, bilateral relations became more dynamic. When both countries gained independence from the British in the 1940s and 1950s, bilateral relations soared to greater heights, expanding in many areas of cooperation. The year 2022 marks the 65th year of Malaysia–India diplomatic relations. Given their long history, both countries have established close bonds in terms of economic and people-to-people contact. India has ranked in the top 10 as Malaysia's trading partner for the last ten years and is among the third-largest Indian diaspora outside of India. However, the authors argue that, despite the long and rich political history, bilateral ties between these countries appear to lack robustness. During the early phase of relations since Malayan independence in 1957, Malaysia–India relations were viewed as "strong and close." There were many reciprocal visits by leaders underscored by a spirit of collaboration and cooperation. However, there is less understanding of the extent and depth of bilateral cooperation, especially during the era of the first prime minister of Malaysia, Tunku Abdul Rahman (1957–1970). The authors discuss several historical events that facilitated Malaysia–India cooperation on significant international issues, particularly during Tunku Abdul Rahman's premiership. The bilateral relationship established during the Tunku-Nehru era of the 1950s and 1960s is significant since it was characterized by a high level of ideological and political consensus and cooperation in confronting Cold War forces. On the economic front, the authors argue that India has challenges in transitioning from the Look East Policy to the Act East Policy and infusing more meaningful content into India's economic interaction with Malaysia and ASEAN in general. Bilateral ties were strained during Dr. Mahathir Mohamad's first and second tenure as Prime Minister. His criticism of India's citizenship law and policy decisions turning Jammu and Kashmir into Union Territories elicited a strong economic response from India—it decided to boycott the purchase of palm oil from Malaysia for several months. These episodes indicate that there are still hurdles to realizing mutual interests between these countries.

The second chapter, Malaysia–India Economic Relations After the End of the Cold War, explores the linkages between India and Malaysia that were evident even before the governments established official ties following Malaya's independence in 1957. The authors claim that although India has always maintained a friendly disposition towards Malaysia, there was no articulation of a distinct policy until the Look East Policy (LEP) was launched in 1992 to formalize India's engagement with ASEAN. Economic ties between Malaysia and India have since been most evident in specific sectors, highlighting that there is room for improvement in others. Palm oil has remained an important trading commodity, even to the point of becoming the deal-breaker between the two countries in recent times. Although there are ongoing challenges in market access in the services sector, in addition to the global crisis caused by Covid-19, bilateral ties are robust with channels of engagement, active and open. The future holds much promise for Malaysia–India economic relations.

Chapter 3, Strengthening Malaysia–India People-to-People (P2P) Connectivity through Tourism, posits that significant economic and socio-cultural dynamics have facilitated relations between India and Malaysia for decades. The socio-cultural aspect has always been viewed as one of the most fascinating and significant dimensions of the Malaysia–India relationship. The author claims that although the centuries-old relationship between Malaysia and India was initiated and sustained by trade, the impact of socio-cultural influence was equally dominant in shaping Malaysia's multiethnic and multicultural façade. In recent years, social and cultural factors have become an important consideration in maintaining bilateral relations between Malaysia and India. The author investigates how socio-cultural elements have brought Malaysia and India closer, particularly in *tourism*. This chapter shows how the process of globalization has intensified the social interactions and connectivity between Malaysia and India.

In the fourth chapter, India–Malaysia Maritime Cooperation: A Missed Opportunity, the author contends that India and Malaysia have a strong maritime bond due to their long-standing proximity and oceanic neighbourhood in the Eastern Indian Ocean Region (EIOR). Despite their differing foreign policy perspectives during the Cold War, both countries have expressed a strong desire for increased maritime security cooperation in the EIOR. The author claims that India and Malaysia maintain a cordial partnership in the maritime domain. However, the critical bearing that requires attention is the need for both countries to draw up effective maritime policies. Maritime security is gaining momentum in the EIOR and has become an area of major significance for many countries. The EIOR concurrently faces several diverse issues requiring coordination and a cooperative approach to mitigate both traditional and nontraditional maritime challenges. Common maritime threats demand their cooperation, though both countries lack engagement, and it is unclear why. The author argues that the positive relations challenged by these maritime threats show the need to identify factors that may discourage the existence, extent, and depth of maritime cooperation between the two oceanic neighbours. An analysis of the issues and challenges in achieving formal commitment between India and Malaysia, prospects of informal commitment, and catalysts for maritime strategic thinking will elicit a more substantial answer to enhancing the robustness of the bilateral relations between the two countries.

Chapter 5, One Identity, Two Realities: Social Issues Among the Sikhs in Malaysia and Punjab, India,' focuses on social issues affecting Sikhs in Malaysia and Punjab, India, discusses the traditional ties between the Sikh communities in Malaysia and India. The authors claim that a society with its cultural ideas and beliefs is not immune to the social difficulties that might threaten the group's stability and harmony. Sikh communities worldwide are also impeded by societal problems that are rarely discussed in public. It is well known that Sikhs worldwide follow a consistent way of life based on the teachings of *Guru Granth Sahib*. Sikhs are structured in an egalitarian system where gender, age, ethnicity, or country disparities are not essential, thanks to the Sikh code of behaviour known as *Sikh Rehat Maryada* (SRM). However, most social issues plaguing the Sikh community are primarily based on the social inequalities that revolve around family institutions. Hence, the authors compare and discuss the social problems experienced by the Sikhs in Malaysia and Punjab, India. Although the Punjabi Sikh ethnicity has many commonalities, particularly in terms of religious identities, such as *Khalsa* and the *5K* symbol, each faces a unique societal scenario. As a minority ethnic group, Sikhs in Malaysia see the plight of familial institutions that play a lesser role in preserving the Punjabi language. On the other hand, despite being the majority in Punjab, the Sikh community suffers a serious issue with drug addiction among its youth. Furthermore, both societies face similar challenges, such as alcoholism, which is especially prevalent among the youth. This shows that Sikhs in both countries do not entirely value and follow the Sikh religion's principles.

The sixth and final chapter is Religious Intolerance in India and Malaysia. The authors claim that India and Malaysia have long been a melting pot of civilizations and cultures, with a broad spectrum of racial, ethnic, and religious groups. However, in recent decades, despite the expressions of accommodation and tolerance of other socioeconomic classes, religious intolerance has increased in India and Malaysia, particularly among religious minorities. Hence, the chapter addresses the primary question of *What went wrong?* in these countries. The authors investigate the type and nature of religious intolerance that religious minorities endure, especially from the perspective of actions taken by state institutions in India and Malaysia. The religious majority in Malaysia are Muslims, whereas the religious majority in India are Hindus. Meanwhile, Malaysia's religious minorities are Hindus, Christians, Buddhists, Taoists and other religions, while India's are made up of Muslims, Christians and other religious groups. The authors argue that there are two types of religious intolerance—*physical* and *nonphysical*. Physical religious intolerance encompasses state-sanctioned mistreatment of minority religious groups and individuals, including arrests and raids, the destruction of religious structures, and restrictions on religious symbolism and attire. While nonphysical religious intolerance includes state restrictions prohibiting conversion activities, prohibiting the use of sacred religious words, safeguarding sacred animals, and prohibiting unsacred animals deemed sensitive. The authors contend that political-economic interests and social identity greatly influence acts of religious intolerance. Hence, the authors propose that building religious tolerance thinking and behaviour is fundamental to fostering societal harmony and political stability.

REFERENCES

Bala Krishnan, Dhesegaan. 2020. "Golden age when Malaysia's ties with India were warm." The STAR, January 28, 2020. https://www.thestar.com.my/opinion/letters/2020/01/28/golden-age-when-malaysias-ties-with-india-were-warm

Izzuddin, Mustafa. 2018. "Malaysia-India relations at a crossroads. Strategic engagement, ethnic politics." Asia and the Pacific Policy Society Policy Forum. April 11, 2018. https://www.policyforum.net/malaysia-india-relations/

Kachiar, Yatharth. 2020. "Will a New Government in Malaysia Reset India Ties? The Muhyiddin government seems keen to thaw the ice, but there are major pitfalls ahead." The Diplomat. April 20, 2020. https://thediplomat.com/2020/04/will-a-new-government-in-malaysia-reset-india-ties/

Ministry of External Affairs (MEA). 2017. "Joint Statement of the India—Malaysia CEO's Forum, New Delhi." March 31, 2017. https://mea.gov.in/bilateral-documents.htm?dtl/28294/Joint+Statement+of+the

Moorthy, Ravichandran. 2016. "Ethnic Indian in Malaysia: History and Issues of Development." In *Contemporary Malaysian Indian: History, Issues, Challenges and Prospects*, edited by Denison Jayasooria and K. S. Nathan, 39–56. KITA: Bangi.

Moorthy, Ravichandran, and Ummadevi, Suppiah. 2012. "Tamils in Malaysia: History, Development and Pluralism." In *Federalism, Democracy and Conflict Resolution*, edited by Arshi Khan and Kushal Pal, 243–265. Delhi, India: Macmillan.

New Straits Times (NST). 2018. "Modi meets Mahathir during stopover in K.L." June 1, 2018. https://www.straitstimes.com/asia/se-asia/modi-meets-mahathir-during-stopover-in-kl

Wheatley, Paul. 1961. *The Golden Khersonese: Studies in the Historical Geography of the Malay Peninsula before A.D. 1500.* Kuala Lumpur: University of Malaya Press.

Winstedt, Richard Olaf. 1935. "A History of Malaya." *Journal of the Malayan Branch of the Royal Asiatic Society*, 13(1) (121): iii–270. http://www.jstor.org/stable/41559833

Chapter 1

Malaysia–India Bilateral Relations

History, Issues, Challenges and Prospects

Suseela Devi Chandran and K. S. Nathan

**INTRODUCTION: EARLY RELATIONS
OF MALAYA–INDIA**

An "Indian era of Malayan history" existed until A.D. 1511, the year Malacca fell to the Portuguese (Wiebe and Mariappen 1979, 2). Most of the Indians who migrated to Malaya in the early years came to trade and undertake commercial activities. In fact, until the Second World War (WW2), the Indian investments in Malaya were not high in magnitude compared to those of the Chinese. Many came on their own from the traditional trading communities, bringing along their own influence of the Indian civilization. Kernial Singh Sadhu (1969, 297) in his analysis of the immigration and settlement of Indians in Malaya stated that, the Indians who came early represented "a powerful and respected commercial, economic and political force." The large-scale immigration of Indians to work on plantations can be attributed to few factors (see Sadhu 1969, Arasaratnam 1970, Wiebe and Mariappen 1979). Among the circumstances that triggered this migration are (i) the hardships experienced by the people in the South Indian states, (ii) the British—who simultaneously took control in India, Ceylon and Malaya—had considerable experience in the running of plantations with the help of Tamil labourers in Ceylon, (iii) the British knew how to manage the Indians, taking cognizance of the easy subservience of the lower caste Indian labourers, and encouraged their coming, (iv) the ways in which, historically and contemporaneously, the Malays were involved primarily in subsistence farming and agriculture, while the Chinese were becoming more clearly identified with urban life, and trade and commercial activities, thus "leaving over" relatively limited resources for work in Malaya's developing plantations, and (v) the continuously rising British dominance in Southeast Asia, which enabled them to encourage the transfer of labour as they saw fit.

The South Indians came to Malaya in great numbers during the latter half of the nineteenth century. They came under many different practical arrangements (Arasaratnam 1970, 10–48; Wiebe and Mariappen 1979, 3–4). Close to half came under the *kangani* pattern of recruitment where selected Indian employees of estates (*kanganis*) traveled back and forth to India, recruiting labour for Malaya's plantations. It should be noted that almost 30 percent of South Indians comprise predominantly Tamilians who also came as free migrants to seek employment in the railways, government departments, and public services, while a minority engaged in business activities. In the public sector, many Indians worked as clerks, technicians, hospital assistants, accountants and cashiers. Malaysian Indians accorded high priority to being trained as doctors, engineers and teachers—hence, there is a disproportionately high percentage of doctors, engineers and teachers in the Malaysian Indian community, which represents only 10 percent of the total Malaysian population.

However, from the perspective of India, relations with Malaya have always been "taken for granted" until the fear of China's expansionism and the danger of spread of communism dictated an adjustment in India's policy towards Malaysia. The following sections recapitulate the evolution of Malaysia's relations with India under the leadership of Malaya's first prime minister, Tunku Abdul Rahman.

2.0 MALAYSIA–INDIA RELATIONS UNDER TUNKU ABDUL RAHMAN

India's relations with Malaysia blossomed during the early 1960s. Malaysia extended its help to India when India faced two major conflicts, i.e., the India-China War (1962) and India-Pakistan conflict (1965). In return, India reciprocated the favour by supporting Malaysia. India lent Malaysia diplomatic support during the Malaysian-Indonesian Confrontation period (known as Konfrontasi), the Afro-Asia meeting and in NAM (Singh and Syeda Sana Rahman 2010, 71).

2.1 Malaysia's Support for India during the Sino-Indian Order Border War

Tunku Abdul Rahman was first among world leaders to condemn the Chinese aggression. During his tour of India in October 1962, he exposed the Chinese motives behind the aggression (Singh 1963: 80). As Malaya then had a large Chinese population, he was cautious and observed that the trouble between India and China "is one which they must consider as between Communist China against democratic India." Malaya supported India's fight against China's communist aggression. The Tunku declared in Singapore on 1 November 1962 that in the event of declaration of war between India and China, Malaya would give "all the support" to India and he decried a half-way policy on this question. On 3 November 1962, a public fund called "Save Democracy Fund" was launched by the Malayan Prime Minister to help India defend herself against China's aggression. A total of USD1 million was collected for the Indian war effort (Abdullah Ahmad 1985, 28). Tunku supported India because of that country's association with the Commonwealth and its faith in democracy, and the shared history of being subjected to communist threat (Sayeed 1968, 236). Tunku believed neutralism was not a guarantee of safety for any country, as India was discovering for itself. In an effort to forestall possible trouble, Tunku emphasized that Malaya was not siding with India against China; rather that it favoured democracy to communism (Abdullah Ahmad 1985, 28). The Indian Prime Minister, Pandit Jawaharlal Nehru, thanked Tunku for his support and said it was significant that Malaya and India renewed the friendship, especially in times of the crisis (Asian Recorder 1962, 4948).

2.2 Malaysia's Support for India in the India-Pakistan Conflict

Another episode which strengthened and exhibited the existence of mutual and friendly ties between Malaysia and India was during the India-Pakistan territorial conflict. In 1965, when hostilities broke out between India and Pakistan on the issue of sovereignty over certain territories of Kashmir, Malaysia adopted a favourable attitude towards India although it followed a policy of conciliation and called both parties to settle the conflict peacefully. Tunku even declared his leadership to mediate on this matter under the auspices of the United Nations (UN) (Ezhilarasi 2000, 295). When Pakistan attacked India on 1 September 1965, the Malaysian representative in the United Nations, Mr. Radhakrishna Ramani, while speaking in the Security Council during the debate on the Indo-Pakistan armed conflict, criticized Pakistan for not only having initiated the conflict but also for its unwillingness to obey the cease-fire call of the Security Council (Sayeed 1968, 237). Mr. Ramani even went to the extent of comparing Pakistan's attack on India with Indonesia's confrontation against Malaysia as follows:

"We in our part of the world have been facing for the last two years this kind of war, infiltration, subversion, sabotage and we can speak with some knowledge learnt in the hard school of experience. " (Ezhilarasi 2000, 288)

2.3 India's Show of Support for Malaysia during the Formation of Malaysia and in Afro-Asian Conference

India's role in the conflict between Indonesia and Malaysia is yet another interesting case to study. India's immediate response on the formation of Malaysia was positive. India was in support of Malaya's idea of the proposed federation, manifested as early as December 1961. *"During a visit by the Yang di-Pertuan Agong of Malaya to India, Vice-President of India Mr. Sarvepalli Radhakrishnan offered his support for the Malaysia plan"* (Arora 1979, 566). India made its stance known during a dinner hosted by Mrs. Lakshmi N. Menon, Minister of State for External Affairs, to the Prime Minister of Singapore. In her speech, Lakshmi Menon welcomed the formation of Malaysia and hoped that it will soon be materialized (Arora 1981, 116). It was on 27 March 1961 Tunku announced in his speech to Foreign Correspondents Association (Singapore) that "Sooner or later Malaysia which cannot stand alone and in isolation should have an understanding with Britain and the people of the territories of Singapore, North Borneo, Brunei and Sarawak and can be brought together in the political and economic cooperation" (Ezhilarasi 2000, 294).

India welcomed this proposal for a variety of reasons. *"First, the emergence of Malaysia would mark the end of the remnants of British colonialism in the region. Secondly, Malaysia offered a sound politically and economically viable alternative to instability in insular Southeast Asia. Thirdly, Singapore's Prime Minister Lee Kuan Yew placed much emphasis on the anti-Communist content of the Malaysia plan during his talks in New Delhi and did suggest that, when viewed from that angle, the proposed federation would be in India's interests"* (Arora 1979, 567). Indonesia opposed this proposal as it was deemed as neo-colonialism in the region. Although India and Indonesia had developed a close political relationship from the late 1940s and both nations were founders of the NAM (along with Yugoslavia and Egypt) in 1961, India decided to be a significant supporter of Malaysia during the Konfrontasi (Brewster 2011, 222). India has always been sympathetic to the British colony of Malaya. India regarded the freedom of the British colonies as "the first thing" and this was in accord with India's policy towards the region both before and since independence. And at the same time, India was grateful to independent Malaya's consistent support during the Indo-Sino War and the Indo-Pakistan conflicts. India also vigorously sponsored a campaign to elect Malaysia to a nonpermanent seat in the United Nations Security Council. Nehru's strong support of Malaysia won him praise from the Prime Minister of Malaysia, Tunku Abdul Rahman, who said Nehru was a person who is "always a vital inspiration to all who love freedom" (Onwimon 1981, 45–46). Mr. Dinesh Singh, Deputy Minister of External Affairs of India, during his visit to Malaysia, claimed that India's support for Malaysia was based on two reasons. Firstly, it would bring independence to a number of countries in the region that were still under the colonial rule, and secondly, the people in the territories concerned were anxious to federate (New Straits Times 1963, 7).

When Malaysia was inaugurated on 16 September 1963, there was a huge demonstration in Indonesia. The demonstration was not only against the formation of Malaysia but also towards the British. Indonesian President Sukarno estranged the trade and economic relations with Malaysia and adopted a policy of "*confrontation*" against Malaysia (Arora 1979, 578). India, however, welcomed the inauguration of Malaysia. In an official message to H. M. theYang di-Pertuan Agong of Malaysia, the President of India conveyed "*to the Government and people of Malaysia the most cordial congratulations of the Government and the people of India*" and "*sincere good wishes for the prosperity and well-being of the new state and for welfare and advancement of the Malaysian people.*" Prime Minister Nehru wrote to the Prime Minister of Malaysia, Tunku Abdul Rahman, to give him his "warm felicitations and greetings on the happy occasion of the inauguration of the Federation of Malaysia" (Arora 1979, 578). The Minister of State for External Affairs of India, Lakshmi Menon, participated in the celebrations on the occasion as India's representative. In the meantime, there were anti-Malaysia disturbances in Jakarta, Indonesia. The Indian Ambassador to Indonesia, Apa B. Pant, offered protection and sheltered the Malayan Ambassador in his house for a night. This clearly showed the closeness and cordial relationships that Malaysia and India had established.

Another event that portrayed India–Malaysia close relations was during the Asian-African Conference. The first large-scale Asian-African or Afro-Asian Conference—also known as Bandung Conference—was a meeting of Asian and African states, most of which were newly independent, which took place on April 18–24, 1955, in Bandung, Indonesia. A total of 29 countries participated at this conference, which was coordinated by Ruslan Abdul Gani, Secretary General of the Indonesian Ministry of Foreign Affairs. The conference's stated aims were to promote Afro-Asian economic and cultural cooperation and to oppose colonialism or neo-colonialism by either the United States or the Soviet Union, or any other imperialistic nations. The conference was an important step towards the crystallization of the Non-Aligned Movement. At the preparatory meeting of the Second Asian-African Conference in 1964 held in Jakarta, Indonesia, India took the initiative to propose Malaysia as a new member. However, given that Indonesia was still in confrontation with Malaysia, it was decided by a consensus to discuss the matter at a subcommittee level. The subcommittee finally decided to postpone this issue, thus leaving an important matter unresolved. Although India failed in securing an invitation for Malaysia, it is worth noticing here that Malaysia and India envisaged good relations towards each other.

India tried hard to postpone the Second Asian-African Conference. This is because India felt that Malaysia should be included in the conference. Because of this firm standpoint that Malaysia should be invited to the conference, there was strong anti-Indian feeling in Indonesia. As Arora (1979, 589) stated, "*It was in this atmosphere of heightened tension in September 1965 that Pakistan chose to strike India with a view of solving the Kashmir question by force.*" During the India-Pakistan outbreak, it was Malaysia's turn to show its full support to India. Recalled by the Prime Minister of Malaysia in October 1966 on the occasion of the visit by the Vice President of India, Mr. Zakir Hussein, "India's help and support too was a great moral booster for us when anti-Malaysia forces went all out to block us from the Algiers conference and nearly succeeded in do so" (Ezhilarasi 2000, 288).

In the 1960s, Malaysia's political relations with India were strong and close. The reciprocal visits by the head of states and government from both nations were apparent. Rajendra Prasad, the President of India then, was the first foreign Head of State to visit Malaya since Malaya became independent in August 1957. The President visited Malaya from 6–8 December 1958. Tunku told the Federal Legislative Council that it was an honour to Malaya to be able to receive and host a distinguished visitor (Asian Recorder 1959, 2435). As a return visit of compliment, Malaya's Paramount Ruler, His Majesty the Yang di-Pertuan Agong, visited India on December 8, 1961. Reflecting the sentiments, the King said that India and Malaya are friends and neighbours and there is no better way than through personal contacts that the relationship can be renewed (Asian Recorder 1962, 4381). During Tunku's visit to India in October 1962, Tunku was conferred the degree of Doctor of Laws (Honoris Causa) by the Aligarh University, India. This degree was conferred to recognize Tunku as the "architect of modern Malaya" (Asian Recorder 1962, 4948). During this period, India also welcomed the establishment of ASEAN and stated that "*such cooperation could help the countries in this region to achieve economic independence and freedom from economic domination*" (Kaul 2001, 53). In May 1968, Prime Minister of India Mrs. Indira Gandhi visited Malaysia. She emphasized that the bilateral relations between both the countries were growing stronger and more meaningful. Mrs.

Gandhi's visit was primarily to cultivate and renew the contacts at the highest levels, to establish and promote bilateral relations and to know the views and problems of countries in the region (Asian Recorder 1968, 8436–8437).

As a whole, Malaysia–India relations during the time of Tunku reflected Malaysia's regard of India as a countervailing power to China. This relationship is nevertheless important because it laid a strong groundwork for Malaysia–India ties.

3.0 MALAYSIA–INDIA: RESPONDING TO STRATEGIC SHIFTS IN THE POST–COLD WAR ERA

Malaysia, like most Southeast Asian countries, always considered India as an important player in the region. In the 1950s and 1960s, India's model of economic development within the framework of a mixed economy combining features of both capitalism and socialism, together with its democratic framework, was not only appreciated by the superpowers, namely, the United States and the Soviet Union, but was also admired by many Southeast Asian countries who sought direction from India for their domestic and foreign policies (Ghosh 2014, 11). As a result of the unexpected wars that India was involved in during 1962 and 1965, the political leadership in New Delhi was forced to abandon Nehru's grandiose plans and concentrate on beefing up its strength to accommodate the country's security needs. For this, India had to depend heavily on the Soviet Union for its defence requirements (Naidu 2000, 153). The growing rift between China and the Soviet Union, and the normalization of relations between China and the US, were considered the beginning of a major shift in the realignment of forces and in the balance of power at the global level. Moreover, in the 1970s and 1980s, India's weak economic growth, in consonant with its lack of control over the strategic alignment emerging in the region, had not only made it quite irrelevant in the affairs of Southeast Asia, but also brought a major divide in their relationship. Thus, it was a combination of factors and events which further contributed to the already waning Indian interests in Southeast Asia.

During this period, the only mode available to India to relate to Malaysia or any other Southeast Asian country was through the Non-Aligned Movement (NAM). However, it was observed that India did not adhere strictly to the principles of NAM, which rejected the idea of joining power blocs. In the 1970s, India had become increasingly dependent on the Soviet Union for diplomatic, economic and military assistance (Mazumdar 2011, 168). When India signed the 1971 Treaty of Peace, Friendship and Cooperation with the Soviet Union and subsequently recognized the Heng Samrin regime in Cambodia, it strained India's relations with most Southeast Asian countries, including Malaysia. It was also difficult for India and Malaysia to establish closer economic relations due to the differences in the economic systems. India's socialist economic model was a closed system, whereas Malaysia's economic system was an open, market-driven and capitalist system. India's economic system did not match Malaysia's open system. Malaysia was also trapped in its own kind of pro-Western, capitalist, democratic mould—which hindered attempts by Malaysia to interact much with India. There was little synergy between both countries, especially in economic aspects. India was also perceived with suspicion by governments of Southeast Asia after its 1974 nuclear test (Mishra 2001, 7). The naval capabilities of India and its build-up in the Andaman and Nicobar Islands posed anxiety for the ASEAN countries, including Malaysia. India was regarded as posing danger to regional security. India's support to the Indochinese communist regime and India's absence from the ASEAN Dialogue meeting in 1980 severed India's influence on the region.

Furthermore, in this period Malaysia was immersed in its own Look East Policy (LEP) to spur economic growth in the 1980s. The LEP was initiated in late 1981, at the beginning of Mahathir's career as the Prime Minister. The policy did not only focus on Japan, but also South Korea and Taiwan. There was much emphasis on developing co-operative endeavours to facilitate the transfer of technology that would benefit both sides. Mahathir wanted Malaysia to emulate the good values of the East, particularly work ethics and innovative skills. Furthermore, during the Cold War period, Malaysia worked closely with ASEAN on nation building. Malaysia was more involved in ASEAN's effort of nation building within the region.

Despite minor irritants during the height of the Cold War, there was no quarrel or major issues between India and Malaysia. Malaysia had no obstacles to establish closer economic, political and strategic links with India. The political-diplomatic relationship with India was cordial and amiable. Although India was left wing and Malaysia was pro West, Malaysia and India maintained a good base in terms of diplomatic relationship.

The end of the Cold War marked a turning point in Indian foreign policy because of the disappearance of the familiar outlook of the post-war world. India was confronted with new opportunities and challenges in the wake of the Cold War and the onset of a new era of globalization. With the collapse of the Soviet Union and the emergence of a new world order, India lost an important ally as the supplier of military hardware, diplomatic protection in the United Nations Security Council in the form of the Soviet veto and its most reliable partner (Mazumdar 2011, 169). The collapse of Soviet Union signified that the foreign policy that India had adopted for the last two decades, depending on the Indo-Soviet Treaty of Peace, Friendship and Cooperation, had become obsolete (Chiriyankandath 2004, 199). Nevertheless, several other developments emerged in the region at the beginning of the 1990s which contributed to the reconfiguration of India's perception of its new security environment (Grare & Mattoo 2001, 124).

First, the tensions and military build-up by the superpowers in the Indian Ocean came to an end. Second, India emerged from the Cold War as a major regional military power, both stronger and self-confident. Third, with the withdrawal of Soviet forces from Afghanistan, India's relations with China and the United States improved markedly. The new atmosphere provided an opportunity for India to reassess and redefine its foreign policy objectives in a realistic and pragmatic manner. Indian analysts and policy makers advocated for a new understanding to be achieved at different structural levels—regionally and globally—to adapt the new geopolitics. The end of the Cold War also marked a turning point in the Indian economy indicating a change of approach based on the liberalization of economy. Mohan (2004) elucidates the important changes in Indian foreign policy during the 1990s, which included the increasing emphasis on economic interests in foreign policy, the abandonment of an idealistic foreign policy symbolized by non-alignment, the primacy of national interests in foreign policy formulations and rejection of anti-Americanism.

It was only after the collapse of the Soviet Union and the end of the Cold War that the government of India was compelled to take a more national-interest-based approach. India's new economic policies demanded a more focused outreach that emphasized trade and commercial undertakings. India adopted some significant changes to adjust the foreign policy orientation to suit the new global environment. Amongst the changes include, apart from relegating the earlier non-aligned-centered policy to the background, a serious attempt was undertaken to delineate the foreign policy priorities from security concerns. Second, an Economic Division was created under the Ministry of External Affairs to give greater economic impetus to India's foreign policy. The third significant initiative that India took was to launch the Look East Policy, aimed to establish closer political links and develop strong economic bonds with Southeast Asian countries (Naidu 2011, 140).

The relations between Malaysia and India started off on a high note, but towards the end of the Cold War, they dwindled to focus more on the political-diplomatic levels only. During the period of Tunku, Malaysia and India had strong and close relationships. Among the factors for the close relationship was the ideological factor—Tunku was against communism, the personal relationship between Nehru and Tunku, and membership in NAM (Non-Aligned Movement), where India was a major advocate. All these factors, one way or another, fostered close bilateral ties. However, as India moved closer towards the Soviet Union, Malaysia slowly drifted away from India. At the same time, Malaysia was also building its relationship with

ASEAN and pursuing the principles of ZOPFAN (Zone of Peace, Freedom and Neutrality).

From Malaysia's perspective, Malaysia was ready to respond to India after the Cold War. Malaysia did not have to wait for the end of the Cold War to strengthen relations with India as trade, investment, political visits were already taking place between Malaysia and India. It is just that the trade did not attain high levels compared to the period after the Cold War. The end of the Cold War also saw the shift in India's economic system, which was similar to the model pursued by Malaysia. Hence there was no problem of divergence between the two economic models. There was a natural flow of trade and investment between the two states, as they operated under the same economic system. Mutuality of interest and system had increased the compatibility between Malaysia and India. Thus, the quantum leap in trade, defence, and people-to-people interactions was only achieved after the Cold War through various MOUs and agreements. This did not take place during the Cold War due to different priorities, especially in India.

At the leadership level, all the Malaysian prime ministers during the Cold War years were also friendly towards India and substantial cooperation took place, especially in terms of law, education, civilian administrative, democracy and defence cooperation. The close bonding established between Nehru and Tunku still underscored a significant aspect in Malaysia–India bilateral relations. Also, at the policy level, there was no friction between Malaysia and India. The ASEAN Charter provided the framework for Malaysia to work with countries in the region. Malaysia did not harbour any ambition to become leader in the region, as it only wanted to work with ASEAN. The political-diplomatic level during the Cold War was stable and high, though it did not inch higher. There was a convergence of views shared between India and Malaysia during the Cold War, such as the principles of Bandung, the politics of the subcontinent on Pakistan and China, and NAM.

To sum up, it can be said that this convergence at the political-diplomatic level could not be translated to other sectors such as in trade, investment, people-to-people ties, and defence cooperation. Bilateral ties remained at a low level despite the positive relationship during the Cold War, even though India had no direct security dispute or military problem with Southeast Asian countries, nor was India viewed as an aggressor in Southeast Asia. In the decades after the Cold War, Malaysia and India generally had a positive relationship, but it did not progress towards a closer, strong and strategic relationship. This could be explained by the fact that New Delhi had other foreign policy priorities away from Southeast Asia, while Malaysia preferred to focus on strengthening ties with its regional neighbours in ASEAN and also on forging new partnerships with rising China. For Malaysia–India relations to progress in new strategic directions, a serious review of the bilateral relationship both in Kuala Lumpur and New Delhi had become necessary, especially in the context of how India's Look East Policy could be re-energized in the first and second decades of the 21st century.

4.0 FROM LOOK EAST TO ACT EAST AND THE MALAYSIA–INDIA STRATEGIC PARTNERSHIP IN THE NAJIB ERA: 2009–2018

India's desire to play a more active role in Southeast Asia since the dawn of the New Millennium clearly was driven by geopolitical as well as national interest considerations. The geopolitical map of Southeast Asia was fast changing with the economic rise of China and the growing political-diplomatic role of ASEAN, whose regional influence was increasingly recognized by all external powers. The consolidation of ASEAN as a regional force was particularly visible in its move towards the establishment of the ASEAN Community by 2015. India was becoming more cognizant of the strategic significance of the three-pronged ASEAN Community in the security (ASC), economic (AEC) and socio-cultural (ASCC) dimensions. Such a regional momentum towards community formation opened up vast opportunities in trade, investment and diplomacy and security engagement by external powers. New Delhi was keenly aware that "Looking East" is not enough, but "Acting East" could well prove vital to the effective promotion of India's national interest in Southeast Asia, including Malaysia. Evidently, the bilateral relationship had to acquire the status of a strategic partnership for India and Malaysia to realize substantial mutual gains. Thus, in the present globalized era marked by the growing impact of economics and technology, there was a growing realization in New Delhi that the way forward lies in recognizing and capitalizing on these new factors and trends in the regional geo-strategic environment.

The movement from a diplomatic-strategic perspective (i.e., from a mere statement of principles and intent) to concrete action in economic, political and military affairs undergirded Prime Minister Modi's approach to Southeast Asia. Modi recognized the importance of ASEAN as the anchor of regional stability and cooperation. The Indian prime minister was equally aware that other external powers, especially China and Japan, were re-configuring their engagement with the regional entity in line with Asia's new security architecture marked by the rise of the two Asian giants (China and India). Malaysia, for its part, was prepared to strengthen political and economic ties with all major powers, including China and India—two Asian powers whose economic strength has been growing over the past two to three decades. Najib Razak was also willing to leverage on the Indian diaspora in Malaysia, a move that was also being pursued under Modi's Act East Policy since 2014.

The Malaysia–India Strategic Partnership was inaugurated in Kuala Lumpur on 27 October 2010 during Prime Minister Manmohan Singh's visit to Malaysia. Both countries wished to leverage on each other's rising political, economic, and diplomatic strengths and provide more substance to bilateral cooperation in the second decade of the 21st century. Key elements of the strategic partnership included the following: (1) more regularized meetings at the highest levels of government to implement agreed upon principles for upgrading the bilateral relationship; (2) increased mutual investment in infrastructure; (3) strengthened cooperation in defence and defence-related industries as well as collaboration on counter-terrorism and cyber security; (4) establishment of machinery for cooperation in energy, oil and gas development, environment, and ICT where India's talents and capabilities could be deployed to benefit Malaysia's ICT sector; and (5) emphasis on the importance of open, transparent and inclusive regional arrangements based on mutuality of interests with ASEAN as the driving force. Both countries welcomed ASEAN-India Dialogue Relations, ASEAN Regional Forum (ARF) and East Asia Summit (EAS) as important regional mechanisms that advance peace, economic growth and stability of the Asia-Pacific region.[1]

This bilateral strategic partnership was further upgraded at the 27th ASEAN Summit in Kuala Lumpur (18–22 November 2015). Both prime ministers, Narendra Modi and Najib Razak, shared many convergent views on the bilateral relationship and also on India's strategic engagement in Southeast Asia. For India's more positive engagement with Malaysia and with ASEAN, New Delhi recognized the need to convert the principles into action—hence the impetus to move quickly from Look East to Act East. The AEP had a compelling strategic dimension: the transformations resulting from new geopolitical developments, especially China's more robust involvement in pursuing its territorial claims in the South China Sea (SCS). As noted by Palit, the AEP "aims to posit India as a prominent regional actor—an objective consistent with the Modi government's ambition of achieving greater global and regional geostrategic influence" (Palit 2016, 82). India and Malaysia shared the view that freedom of navigation in the SCS was upheld by the UN Conference on the Law of the Sea (UNCLOS). The UN treaty specifically prohibits nationalization of international waters and sea lanes vital to global commerce, shipping and trade. At the bilateral level, the renewed Malaysia–India Strategic Partnership, in conjunction with PM Modi's attendance at the ASEAN Summit in Kuala Lumpur (20–22 November 2015), reiterated greater collaboration in specific areas and sectors to strengthen the connection between the government and business sectors in both countries. India's IRCON will expand investment in railway development in Malaysia, while Malaysian companies will invest further in building roads and infrastructure in two Indian states: Rajasthan and Andhra Pradesh. Two other areas identified for enhancing collaboration were counter-terrorism and cyber security.[2] Nevertheless, it should be noted that when AEP was formally announced in 2014, Indo-ASEAN trade stood at $67.8 billion and accounted for only 2.7 percent of ASEAN's total trade and about 9.4 percent of India's total trade.[3] India also has a continuing trade deficit with Malaysia. India is ranked 10th in the list of top 10 trading partners of Malaysia. In 2017, India's imports from Malaysia were valued at US$5.53 billion, while its exports to Malaysia totaled US$8.90 billion, resulting in a trade deficit of US$3.36 billion.[4] Both Modi and Najib have indicated their commitment to improve the overall trade balance.

5.0 MAHATHIR'S SECOND TENURE AS PRIME MINISTER: EMERGING STRAINS IN BILATERAL RELATIONS

The foregoing discussion was premised on the bourgeoning relationship between India and Malaysia, especially under the premiership of Najib Razak and Narendra Modi. However, the change of government in Malaysia following the May 9, 2018, General Election, which witnessed the return of former prime minister and nonagenarian Mahathir Mohamad, appears to have put some brakes on this strategic partnership. Under the leadership of this second-time PM, the evidence so far indicates that the India–Malaysia nexus has not been sufficiently prioritized. Mahathir's comments on Jammu and Kashmir in the UN stating that India had invaded these territories were not well received by New Delhi, which claimed that Mahathir's "statement" was "not based on facts."[5] Moreover, another irritant in bilateral relations is the continued presence in Malaysia of Islamic hate preacher Zakir Naik, who is wanted by Indian authorities on money laundering charges and for causing religious discord in India. Moreover, the Islamic preacher has made offensive remarks against Malaysians of Chinese and Indian ethnic origin, thus directly interfering in the internal affairs of Malaysia. To date, Malaysia has not responded positively to India's request to extradite Zakir Naik, who has been given permanent residence by the previous BN (National Front) government of Najib Razak. PM Mahathir has been reluctant to deport this hate preacher despite calls from his own ruling coalition (Pakatan Harapan, or Alliance of Hope).[6] These two episodes appear to have impacted negatively on Malaysia's export of palm oil to India in recent months.[7]

It is instructive to note that India is the world's largest importer of edible oils and was the largest buyer of Malaysian palm oil in the first nine months of 2019. The country imported 3.91 million tonnes, or 27.9 percent of Malaysia's total palm oil exports over that period.[8]

In this regard, it is noteworthy that an earlier episode in bilateral relations occurred during Mahathir's first inning as Prime Minister from July 1981 until October 2003. In the final year of his tenure, an incident in which Malaysian police reportedly abused Indian IT professionals had the effect of marring the bilateral relationship. In March 2003, Malaysian police arrested 270 IT professionals residing in the Palm Court apartments in Brickfields, now the new Little India. The Malaysian authorities claimed that these IT workers had improper or insufficient valid documentation for their stay and work in Malaysia. At that material time, around 40,000 Indian expatriates were working in Malaysia, including information technology professionals, engineers, doctors, academics and executives involved in joint ventures. The strong displeasure against police brutality expressed by Indian High Commissioner Veena Sikri resulted in an apology from the Malaysian government.[9] This episode, coupled with another on 25 November 2007 when Malaysian police used tear gas to dismiss thousands of protesting Malaysians of Indian ethnic origin over perceived socio-economic marginalization and discrimination, did little to help improve bilateral relations.[10] In the wake of this incident, leaders of the Hindu Rights Action Force (HINDRAF) called on India to impose trade sanctions on Malaysia to pressurize the latter to adopt affirmative policies to uplift the conditions of its citizens of Indian origin.[11] All three episodes under the Mahathir Administration tend to produce the cumulative view that the Malaysian PM does harbour some undisclosed prejudices against India although his paternal origins are traceable to Kerala in South India.

6.0 CONCLUSION: CHALLENGES AND PROSPECTS

India and Malaysia have several reasons to foster cooperation in the second decade of the 21st century and beyond. Both countries have gone through some rough patches in their bilateral relationship, with Malaysia harbouring negative perceptions of India during the Cold War, and India expressing strong reservation of Malaysia's rough treatment in March 2003 of Indian IT professionals working in Kuala Lumpur.

Nevertheless, the situation has improved substantially since 2009 under Malaysia's sxth prime minister, Najib Razak (2009–2018). High-level visits by both sides were initiated, culminating in Prime Minister Najib's visit to India in January 2010 and Prime Minister Manmohan Singh's visit to Malaysia later in October—both events setting the stage for strengthening bilateral relations, including upgrading the defence and security dimensions. The changed perceptions towards a more positive approach were clearly being driven by current trends in the regional environment and national interest priorities.

The Modi Government under the Act East Policy has viewed the Indian diaspora in Malaysia/Southeast Asia as a "strategic asset" in promoting not just India's foreign policy goals but also working to the mutual advantage of both nations. However, the Mahathir era (1981–2003 and May 2018 to present), unlike the Najib era, has indicated that there are clearly some challenges that lie ahead in utilizing the diasporic dimension for mutual advantage. In contrast to Mahathir's foreign policy priorities, both Modi and Najib recognize the strategic role of the Indian diaspora in Malaysia, numbering over 2 million or constituting 7–8 percent of the country's current population of 32 million.[12] These challenges may well recede in the post-Mahathir era when a more positive review of relations by Kuala Lumpur can be expected—in the not-too-distant future. India and Malaysia have much to gain in strengthening economic cooperation. Both countries have huge talents to share for mutual benefit, with India contributing significantly in IT, infrastructure via IRCON[13] and also in medicine and capacity building, especially in disaster relief, counter-terrorism and cyber security. On the Malaysian side, IJM[14] has been actively involved in building roads, airports, hotels, residences, and other infrastructure following the opening of India since 1991.

The Cold War era of international relations when both Malaysia and India shared similar ideological and political perspectives has now given way to more pragmatic assessments in pursuing foreign policy goals. The rapid pace of globalization, technological change, and expanding multipolarity would tend to drive rational actors to advocate foreign policies underpinned less by ideological and self-serving motives and more by pragmatism that can genuinely advance the national interest. This would most certainly entail a more judicious and strategic use of soft power and smart power—a dimension in which both India and Southeast Asia are likely to excel in the coming decades, including empowering the Indian diaspora for mutual gain.

Under conditions of globalization, the state's role in managing its fallouts and by-products cannot be underestimated. Inasmuch as Malaysia's first prime minister (Tunku Abdul Rahman) and India's first prime minister (Jawahrlal Nehru) had a significant role in promoting good bilateral relations during the Cold War era, the role of Mahathir Mohamad and Najib Razak on the Malaysian side, and Manmohan Singh and Narendra Modi on the other in the post–Cold War era—all affirm the important role the state has played and continues to play in either strengthening or weakening the bilateral relationship. Nevertheless, despite the initiation of the Act East Policy, much works needs to be done to increase India's economic engagement with Malaysia/ASEAN.

The current apparently difficult phase in in state-to state relations between India and Malaysia is not expected to endure post Mahathir. The institutional linkages already established, together with a strong convergence of strategic interests, especially economic, are likely to resurge in the post-Mahathir era when the Malaysia–India Strategic Partnership will likely be fully revived to promote the national interests of two Asian states with strong historical and civilizational links spanning several centuries.

REFERENCES

Abdullah Ahmad. 1985. *Tengku Abdul Rahman and Malaysia's Foreign Policy 1963–1970*. Kuala Lumpur: Berita Publishing Sdn. Bhd.

Arasaratnam, S. 1970. *Indians in Malaysia and Singapore*. Kuala Lumpur: Oxford University Press.

Arora, B. D. 1979. India, Indonesia, and the emergence of Malaya. *International Studies*, 18(4) (Oct.–Dec.): 563–593.

Arora, B. D. 1981. *Indian-Indonesia relations*. New Delhi: Asian Educational Services.

Asian Recorder. 1959. January 1–9. *The Hindu and The Straits Times, Singapore*: 2435–2436.

Asian Recorder. 1962. January 22–28. *The Statesman and The Hindustan Times*: 4381

Asian Recorder. 1962. November 19–25. *The Hindustan Times, The Straits Times, Singapore*: 4948.

Asian Recorder. 1965, October 29–November 4. *The Statesman, The Hindu, The Times of India, New Straits Times, Singapore*: 6748.

Asian Recorder. 1968, July 22–28. *The Straits Times, Singapore, The Malayan Mail, Kuala Lumpur and The Hindu, Madras*: 8436–8437.

Asian Recorder. 1970. March 19–25. *The Statesman, The Straits Times*: 9446.

Brewster, D. 2011. The relationship between India and Indonesia: An evolving security partnership? *Asian Survey*, 51(2) (March/April): 221–244.

Chiriyankandath, J. 2004. Realigning India: Indian foreign policy after the Cold War. *The Roundtable: The Commonwealth Journal of International Affairs, 93*(374): 199–211.

Ezhilarasi, M. 2000. Indo-Malaysia (Malaya) relations. In *Government and Politics of Asian Countries* (Vol. 8), ed. Grover, V. New Delhi: Deep & Deep Publications Pvt. Ltd.

Ghosh, A. 2014. *India-Malaysia relations in the post-Cold War period: From indifference to cordiality*. India: Minerva.

Grare, F., & Mattoo, A. 2001. *India and ASEAN: The politics of India's Look East Policy*. New Delhi: Manohar Publishers.

Kaul, M. M. 2001. ASEAN-India relations during the Cold War. In *India and ASEAN: The politics of India's Look East Policy*, eds. Grare, F., & Matoo, A. New Dehli: Lardson Publishers Pvt. Ltd.

Mazumdar, A. 2011. India's search for a post-Cold War foreign policy: Domestic constraints and obstacles. *India Quarterly*, 67(2): 165–182.

Mishra, P. P. 2001. India-Southeast Asian relations: An overview. *Teaching South Asia: An Internet Journal of Pedagogy*, 1(1): 105–115.

Mohan, R. C. 2004. *Crossing the Rubicon: The shaping of India's new foreign policy*. New York: Palgrave Macmillan.

Naidu, G. V. C. 2000. *Indian Navy and Southeast Asia*. New Delhi: The Institute for Defence Studies and Analyses (IDSA).

Naidu, G. V. C. 2011. India and Southeast Asia: An analysis of the Look East Policy. In *India and ASEAN: Partners at Summit*, ed. Rao, P. V. Singapore: ISEAS & KW Publishers Pvt. Ltd.

New Straits Times. 1963. Two reasons why India supports Malaysia and will continue to do so. 22 May: 7.

Onwimon, S. 1981. *India's relations with the ASEAN countries, 1966–1975: A transaction analysis.* PhD diss., University of Pennsylvania, USA, University Microfilms International.

Palit, Amitendu. 2016. India's Act East Policy and Implications for Southeast Asia. *Southeast Asian Affairs*: 81–91.

Pathmanathan, M., & Lazarus, D. 1984. *Winds of Change: The Mahathir Impact on Foreign Policy*. Kuala Lumpur: Eastview Productions Sdn. Bhd.

Sandhu, K. S. 1969. *Indians in Malaya: Some aspects of their immigration and settlement (1786–1957)*. Cambridge: Cambridge University Press

Sayeed, K. B. 1968. Southeast Asia in Pakistan's foreign policy. *Pacific Affairs, XLI* (2 Summer): 230–244.

Singh, S., & Syeda Sana Rahman. 2010. India-Singapore relations: Constructing a "New" bilateral relationship. *Contemporary Southeast Asia, 32*(1): 70–97.

Singh, V. 1963. The reactions of Southeast Asian countries. *International Studies*, 5(1–2) (July–Oct.): 80–84.

Wiebe, P. D., & Mariappen, S. 1979. *Indian Malaysians: The view from the plantation*. Durham, N.C,: Carolina Academic Press.

NOTES

1. Ministry of External Affairs, Government of India. "Joint Statement on the Framework for the India-Malaysia Strategic Partnership." https://mea.gov.in/bilateral-documents.htm?dtl/4764/Joint+Statement+on+the+Framework+for+the+IndiaMalaysia+Strategic+Partnership (Accessed: 13-1-2020).

2. Ministry of External Affairs, Government of India. "Joint Statement on enhanced Malaysia-India Strategic Partnership" (November 23, 2015): https://mea.gov.in/bilateral-documents.htm?dtl/26057/Joint+Statement+on+enhanced+MalaysiaIndia+Strategic+Partnership+November+23+2015 (Accessed: 10-1-2020).

3. Trisha Ray, "India's Act East Policy: A Track Record and Recommendations for the Future," South Asia Program at Hudson Institute: http://www.southasiaathudson.org/new-page-23 (Accessed: 2-8-2019).

4. Trade Promotion Council of India: Country Profile—Malaysia, 18 February 2019: https://www.tpci.in/blogs/country-profile-malaysia/ (Accessed: 10-1-2020).

5. "What Is the Link between Palm Oil and the Kashmir Dispute?" BBC News, 1 January 2020: https://www.bbc.com/news/world-asia-50317980 (Accessed: 5-1-2020).

6. "Time to deport Zakir, says Tawfik," *STAR ONLINE,* 21 August 2019: https://www.thestar.com.my/news/nation/2019/08/21/time-to-deport-zakir-says-tawfik.

7. Mohamed Tawfik Ismail is the son of former Malaysian Deputy Prime Minister Dr. Ismail Abdul Rahman, who served in this capacity from 1970 to 1973.

8. "Speculation to boycott Malaysia palm oil will boost traders' margin," *The Malaysian Reserve*, 24 October 2019: https://themalaysianreserve.com/2019/10/24/speculation-to-boycott-malaysia-palm-oil-will-boost-traders-margin/ (Accessed: 31-10-2019).

9. "Malaysia to apologise to India over police arrests: report," *Daily News* (22 March 2003): http://www.dailynews.lk/2003/03/22/wor03.html (Accessed: 31 October 2019).

10. "India says Hindraf crackdown a 'source of concern,'" *Malaysiakini,* 1 December 2007: http://www.malaysiakini.com/news/75540 (Accessed: 31-10- 2019).

11. P. Waytha Moorthy, president of Hindu Rights Action Force (Hindraf), asks India to impose sanctions on Malaysia: https://tamilnation.org/diaspora/malaysia /071125protest.htm#P_Waytha_Moorthy, 6 December 2007 (Accessed: 20-12-2019).

12. For details, see K. S. Nathan, "The Indian Diaspora in Southeast Asia as a Strategic Asset of India's Foreign and Security Policy," *Diaspora Studies*, Vol. 8, No. 2, 2015, pp. 120–131.

13. IRCON is the acronym for Indian Railway Construction Company Limited.

14. IJM is the acronym for the merger between three medium-sized local construction companiesIGB Construction Sdn Bhd, Jurutama Sdn Bhd and Mudajaya Sdn Bhd, formed in 1983.

Chapter 2

Malaysia–India Economic Relations After the End of the Cold War

Angelina Gurunathan and Ravichandran Moorthy

INTRODUCTION

India's ancient trade roots in Southeast Asia go all the way back to the sixth century in what is now known as Malaysia. The sixth-century Indian traders waited for the monsoons to change at the ports of the Kedah coast, which is a northern state in Malaysia. The ports eventually became settlements even as they became regional trading hubs for the neighbouring region (Singh 2009). One such famous entrepot was the Bujang Valley in Kedah. At that time, Kedah was part of the Srivijaya Kingdom and was a key trading point for the Southeast Asian region as well as for trading between India and China. This continued until Malacca supplanted the Bujang Valley as an entrepot complex in the fourteenth century. Archeological evidence also shows that apart from interactions necessitated by trade, other independent interactions also existed between Southeast Asia and India (Murphy 2018). Trade between India and Southeast Asia continued to expand from being driven mainly by Burma, Indonesia, Malaysia, Thailand and Indochina, from whom India mainly imported oil, tin, rubber, rice and timber after the second world war (Singh 2009). India now has substantial trade ties with almost all ASEAN member states. Malaysia and India have had among the most significant and longstanding economic partnerships in the region. This chapter aims to provide a summary of the key aspects of Malaysia–India economic ties over the last three decades. In the first section, India's economic relationship with the Association of Southeast Asian Nations (ASEAN) is outlined to provide the background against which India's bilateral relations are established with Malaysia. The following sections discuss Malaysia–India economic ties by focusing on Malaysia's construction sector in India and the bilateral Free Trade Agreement (FTA) between the two countries. These sections aim to highlight the success stories before moving on to some of the more pertinent, on-going as well as recent challenges experienced in the bilateral economic ties in the next section. In conclusion, it is evident that certain high-profile personalities within Malaysia have been instrumental in both the strengthening and weakening of ties with India. However, having been forged at multiple levels of interactions since antiquity, the ties that bind both countries have remained strong, with the path ahead paved with untapped opportunities.

INDIA–ASEAN TIES: AN OVERVIEW

Malaysia was a founding member of ASEAN. The regional organization was formed in 1967, driven mainly by concerns over regional security. The leaders who founded ASEAN from the free market economies of Indonesia, Malaysia, Thailand, Singapore and the Philippines had perceived the necessity of a political entity of cooperation to safeguard their nations. The region was in volatile circumstances as it faced security threats in the form of intra-regional confrontations and territorial disputes as well as communist insurgency backed by external powers who were key protagonists of the Cold War. The founding fathers, while declaring the formation of ASEAN, among others, desired "to establish a firm foundation for common action to promote regional cooperation in South-East Asia in the spirit of equality and partnership and thereby contribute towards peace, progress and prosperity in the region" (ASEAN 1967). During the Cold War, India and ASEAN countries found themselves on opposing sides of the global dichotomy. India's diplomatic support for Vietnam during Vietnam's 1978–1979 invasion of Cambodia went against the sentiments of ASEAN (Blank et al. 2015). Nevertheless, the dynamics in the relations between India and ASEAN took a positive turn eventually in the 1990s with the collapse of the Soviet Union that ended the Cold War in 1991.

In 1991, when India underwent the dramatic change in its foreign policy directions and liberalized its economy, India recognized the importance of ASEAN to the country's national interests. Against the backdrop of increasing regionalism that was starting to create small trade blocs around the world, India saw opportunities in ASEAN. The members of ASEAN who were open to foreign investment attracted multinational corporations (MNCs) mainly from Japan, the US, the UK as well as South Korea, who in turn set out to avail themselves of the benefits of lower cost of production and integrated regional production network. For the period between 1965 and1990, East Asian growth performance was outstanding and this was credited to the eight high-performing Asian economies. Among the eight, four were members of ASEAN. They were Singapore, which was also one of the "Four Tigers," and Indonesia, Malaysia as well as Thailand that were among the newly industrialising economies (NIEs) of Southeast Asia (Birdsall et al. 1993). The region was naturally blessed with the Malacca Straits, which was a major trade route, and had commodifiable resources that contributed greatly to the rapid industrialization that was happening mainly in Malaysia, Indonesia, the Philippines and Thailand beginning in the 1970s. These countries started to emulate the success paths of the East Asian economies of Japan, Korea and Taiwan. The export-oriented policies instituted were greatly supported by foreign direct investments coming from those developed East Asian economies, the developed Western nations in Europe as well as from the US (Nehru 2011).

THE RCEP CHALLENGE

ASEAN has remained important to India; it is the core of India's Look East Policy (LEP), which was later rebranded as the Act East Policy (AEP), as well as India's Indo-Pacific Vision announced in 2018. India's economic ties remain the main component of its partnership with the regional body. The Free Trade Agreement on Goods between ASEAN and India (ASEAN-India Trade in Goods Agreement [AITIGA]) came into force in 2010, and this was followed by ASEAN-India Trade in Investment Agreement (AITIIA) in 2014 and the ASEAN-India Trade in Services Agreement (AITISA) in 2015. Between 2012 and 2019, India was a part of the Regional Comprehensive Economic Partnership (RCEP) negotiations comprising ten ASEAN member states and its six dialogue partners of Australia, China, India, Japan, Korea and New Zealand. India then withdrew from the negotiations in November 2019 (MEA 2019b) in light of concerns over the impact that the possible flooding of dairy goods from Australia and New Zealand would have on its farmers, and the exacerbation of India's trade deficit by the influx of Chinese manufactured goods (Anon 2019d).

India had till 2018, prior to its withdrawal from RCEP, signed on to 14 FTAs. Overall, it was found that the utilization rate of the preferential tariff rates made possible via these FTAs among Indian businesses was low, registering at a level between 5 and 25 percent. NITI Aayog, a think-tank of the Indian Government, questioned the benefits of the FTAs for the Indian economy when exports to India's FTA partners had failed to outperform exports to India's non-FTA partners. India's FTA with ASEAN also was found to have had the biggest trade impact on India. Trade deficit with ASEAN had increased after the FTA had come into force in 2011 and this was largely alluded to the fact that India had offered much more in the agreement compared to its ASEAN partners. India also was not able to obtain the intended level of reciprocity in the services sector to compensate for the inadequacies the country felt subjected to within the goods sector (Saraswat, Priya, and Ghosh 2018). These arguments were also reflected as part of the reasons for India's withdrawal from RCEP (ASEAN 2019a).

India's economic growth is highly dependent upon its robust services sector. The sector contributes over half of India's gross value added (MOF 2020). India's approach has always been an offensive one when it came to negotiating for the liberalization of the services sector in FTAs. India has a very uncompetitive domestic industrial sector, making manufacturers from ASEAN a threat. Services trade liberalization, which also touches on investment liberalization, as well as freer movement of professionals, among others, are areas where regulatory practices and requirements are too divergent among ASEAN states. There are on-going challenges in mutual recognition of qualifications and standards in those areas. The services sector also touches on the sensitive area of public service such as health and education as well. This inevitably creates an impasse in the trade negotiations process with India (Basu Das 2018).

The services sector, which is uniquely intertwined in most aspects of a society, unlike the goods sector, is subject to heavy regulation and supervision by the government. So, given the myriad of legal domestic considerations in each ASEAN state, India's attempt to satisfactorily liberalize the services sector through RCEP had been unsuccessful. India's domestic industries and the welfare of its farmers in the agriculture sector were also too huge a political risk to ignore as well (Anon 2019d). In line with the above, India and ASEAN have agreed to the review of the ASEAN-India Trade in Goods Agreement to address the imbalances that India has highlighted for rectification (ASEAN 2019b). The review is a critical aspect of India–ASEAN economic ties moving forward in the absence of RCEP.

MALAYSIA–INDIA ECONOMIC TIES

By the time India launched the LEP in 1992, and formalized its engagements with ASEAN, Malaysia's economy had already undergone some major transformations. Until the 1960s, Malaysia's economy was labor-driven and commodity dependent and it steadily grew into an investment-driven and manufacturing-dependent economy by the 1990s. Malaysia's rapid economic growth started in the 1980s. It had a short dizzy spell during 1985–1986 property market depression but picked up pace again right through the mid-1990s.

The period was an important time for Malaysia's economy, which was making the seminal shift from an agriculture-based economy to one based on manufacturing and industry. For much of the 1990s prior to the Asian Financial Crisis of 1997/1998, Malaysia's growth rate averaged 9 percent annually. Expenditure was heavy on infrastructure, and the volume of manufactured exports, notably electronic goods and electronic components, increased rapidly. Malaysia entered into the upper-middle-income country bracket in the 1990s, and this was also when Malaysia started witnessing the rise of many skyscrapers, including the iconic Twin Towers, which was completed in 1998 (National Economic Advisory Council Malaysia 2010; Anon 2018).

Footprints

Over the years there have been several iconic Malaysian business ventures in India that have given a boost to bilateral economic ties. None of the footprints have been as widely spread and deeply entrenched as those made by Malaysia's construction companies. The construction industry in Malaysia came of age after the successful completion of Malaysia's North-South Highway in 1994. This experience served well for the country's construction industry to venture into international markets, particularly in Asia. Malaysia's former Works Minister Datuk Seri S. Samy Vellu, who was an active proponent of Malaysian construction in India, played a key role in bringing Malaysian companies to India (CIDB Malaysia 2015). He was later made Malaysia's special envoy on infrastructure to India and South Asia in 2011 (Anon 2011b; 2011c). This special appointment carrying the status of a full Minister was indeed a clear reflection of the importance to leverage on the rapport that was already built by Samy Vellu during his time as the Works Minister. Indeed, this was critical because India's rapid growth and expansion necessitated infrastructure developments in a large scale across the subcontinent. The opportunities were immense and Malaysia keenly pursued them (Anon 2011a). The efforts made bore fruit, and it was the first time that a foreign company had a stake in India's road project involving Malaysia's United Infrastructure Resources. The company was part of the consortium that was made up of India's Gayathri Construction Company, to which the Andhra Pradesh government awarded the Nellore bypasss project in 2013 (Shivkumar 2013). Samy Vellu's special envoy position came to a halt in 2018 after Malaysia saw the change in the Malaysian Government for the first time in history since independence (Ong 2018). Nevertheless, Malaysia's construction companies have been steadily gaining stronger footing in India with notable Malaysian companies in the sector in India including IJM, Sunway, Gamuda, WCT Engineering, UEM and Mudajaya (MIDA 2010). Many opportunities across India have continued to open up for Malaysia in the infrastructure sector, including for the development of infrastructure in India's Tier-II cities such as Faridabad, Cuttack, Amritsar, Jamshedpur, Kochi, Jammu, and Bikaner (Anon 2017a).

During Prime Minister Najib Razak's official visit to India in April 2017 to mark 60 years of diplomatic relations between the two countries, there was an exchange of 31 business Memoranda of Understanding (MOUs) with combined investments estimated at USD35.99 billion (RM159.26 billion). These MOUs were related to port construction, highway construction, a solar power plant, development of a smart city and technology park, a regasification terminal project, coconut and palm oil development, and higher learning education. There was also an emphasis on promoting trade and investment by SMEs between the two countries for a more inclusive economic growth. SME Corp Malaysia and the National Small Industries Corporation (NSIC), India, are the focal agencies to facilitate SMEs from both countries to do cross-border businesses (MITI 2017).

India is also among the top 20 investors for Malaysia. According to data available from the Malaysian Investment Development Authority (MIDA), as of 2019 India had embarked on at least 135 manufacturing projects with Malaysia registering an investments value of RM5.5 billion. They are mainly in the textiles and textile products, chemical and chemical products, paper and printing, non-metallic mineral products, electronics and electrical products, and basic metal products. Notable Indian companies with footprints in Malaysia and who have made Malaysia their manufacturing base are Reliance Group, RP Chemical, Ranbaxy and Tamco Switchgear. Indian firms who have ventured into Malaysia's services sector include ICICI Bank Limited, Wipro, Infosys and Tata Consultancy, Sky Blue Media and Manipal International (MIDA 2019). India's iconic state-owned IRCON, which specializes in railway construction, has been in operation in Malaysia since 1988 and was awarded a landmark deal for the double tracking of the railway line from Seremban to Gemas worth US$1 billion in 2008 (Anon 2008). Until September 2019, IRCON has been involved in 15 projects that entailed 580 kilometers of track rehabilitation and approximately 298 kilometers of new lines (MEA 2020a).

Malaysia–India Comprehensive Economic Cooperation Agreement

In terms of bilateral trade between Malaysia and India in the post–Cold War period, total trade has been on an upward trend. Trade data from Malaysia's Department of Statistics indicates that in 1990, total trade between Malaysia and India stood at USD690 million, and in 1995 it was at USD1.3 billion and rose to USD2.6 billion in 2000. Malaysia's main exports to India during this period were palm oil, crude petroleum, iron and steel products, transport equipment and electronics and electrical products. Imports from India were mainly electronics and electrical products, textiles, manufactures of metal, machinery and equipment, chemical and chemical products, and iron and steel products. This upward trend in trade continued modestly and peaked in 2008 with total trade registered hitting the USD 10 billion mark. In 2010, when the Malaysia-India Comprehensive Economic Cooperation (MICECA) was signed, Malaysia and India set a trade target of achieving bilateral trade of USD15 billion by 2015 (Anon 2010). This target was not met due to the global economic slowdown and the decline in commodity prices. The deadline for the target was later moved to the year 2020 (Department of Statistics Malaysia 2021; Anon 2017b).

This target was achieved two years ahead of the deadline. Statistics from the Malaysian side indicated that total trade between India and Malaysia had already reached the target in 2018 with total trade registering at US$15.5 billion. This figure stood at US$15.1 billion in 2019, when India was the seventh largest export destination for Malaysia, and tenth largest import source. Trade remained in favor of Malaysia in 2019, with exports to India totaling US$9.3 billion and imports from India to Malaysia totaling US$5.8 billion. Bilateral trade between Malaysia and India, however, experienced a reduction in 2020 to US$13.1 billion owing to disruptions to the global supply chain in light of the Covid-19 pandemic. Nevertheless, India remained among the top 10 countries for Malaysia's exports and imports with total trade registering a surplus for Malaysia. In 2020, exports to India totaled US$7.2 billion and imports from India to Malaysia totaled US$5.9 billion (Department of Statistics Malaysia 2021).

An important aspect of the Malaysia–India bilateral trading partnership is the Malaysia-India Comprehensive Economic Cooperation Agreement, which came into effect on July 1, 2011, covering goods, services and investment. This came right after the ASEAN-India Trade in Goods Agreement (AITIGA) came into effect in 2010. Both Malaysia and India have given the other ASEAN plus commitments in Trade in Goods, and WTO plus commitments in Trade in Services. In Trade in Goods, for example, under MICECA, fewer products have been placed on the exclusion lists of both countries than the number of products excluded under AITIGA. Under AITIGA Malaysia excluded 898 products while India excluded 1,298. Under MICECA, Malaysia excluded 838 products while India excluded 1,225 products. In terms of trade in services, foreign equity (Indian) shareholding has been allowed in 91 sub-sectors of the Malaysian services sector, whereas Malaysians have been allowed as foreign equity shareholders in 84 services sub-sectors in India (MITI 2020). The services sector is an area where India has offensive interest and Malaysia has provided significant offers in accounting and auditing, architecture, engineering services, medical and nursing, and computer-related services (MEA 2020b). In the same way, Malaysia's offensive interest in India is its exports of palm oil to the subcontinent. India is the world's largest consumer of palm oil, and to get greater access into this market Malaysia has been competing with the largest producer of palm oil, which is Indonesia. Through MICECA, Malaysia had negotiated for better market access through preferential tariffs for its palm oil compared to what was offered by India to Indonesia through AITIGA (MITI 2011). This has effectively made Malaysia's palm oil entering India with a more competitive rate compared to Indonesia's palm oil (Abas 2019).

Malaysia is eyeing to gain a bigger share of India's market with the reduction of import duty by a further 4 and 9 percent for Malaysia's crude and refined palm oil, respectively, which took effect on January 1, 2019, as agreed upon through MICECA. India imports over 9 million tonnes of palm oil annually, and in 2019, a record high of 4.4 million tonnes of palm oil was imported from Malaysia (Jadhav and Thukral 2020). Indonesia, on its part, is also pursuing a greater share of India's palm oil market as it continues to push for a bilateral FTA with India. Negotiations for a Comprehensive Economic Cooperation between India and Indonesia were launched in 2011, a year after AITIGA came into force (MEA 2020c). After a decade of insignificant progress, there now seems to be a renewed vigor to push ahead with India–Indonesia CECA negotiations. This renewal has been credited to firstly, Malaysia's expanding share in India's palm oil market which Indonesia seeks to restrain, and secondly, India's desire to reduce its dependency on Malaysia's palm oil given the remarks made by Malaysia's Prime Minister Tun Mahathir Mohamed at the United Nations General Assembly (UNGA) in 2019 (Jha 2020; Anon 2020d).

Speed Bumps on the Road

Tun Mahathir, who was in his second stint as the country's premier in September 2019, openly criticized India's actions with regard to the revocation of the special status of Jammu and Kashmir. In his speech Mahathir referred to India's actions as invading and occupying Jammu and Kashmir and that those actions were wrong regardless of the reasons cited for them by India (Anon 2019b). The remarks, which were made at a significantly important global platform such as UNGA, strongly suggested Malaysia's departure from its usual adherence of neutrality over the internal affairs of its strategic partners (Kachiar 2020). Mahathir's action at UNGA 2019, triggered a chain of reactions. India's Ministry of External Affairs responded indicating that the Malaysian Government should take into account the relations between Malaysia and India, and that remarks such as those made at

UNGA 2019 should be ceased (Anon 2019a). Soon after MEA once again, in response to Mahathir's subsequent criticism over the amendments made to India's Citizenship Bill in December 2019, issued an official statement asking Mahathir to refrain from commenting on India's internal affairs and summoned Malaysia's top diplomat in Delhi (MEA 2019a; Anon 2019f).

Concerns over the possible impact of Mahathir's statements on Malaysia's trade, particularly over Malaysia's palm oil exports to India, saw Malaysia's Minister of Plantation Industries and Commodities swiftly indicating that Malaysia was already looking into increasing imports of sugar and buffalo meat from India (Anon 2019e). This came after India's major trade association, the Mumbai-based Solvent Extractors' Association (SEA), called for a boycott of Malaysia's palm oil in October 2019 (Anon 2019c). In India, SEA's calls were opposed by the Tamil Nadu Congress Committee (TNCC) citing that such a move had the potential of eventually hurting India's own, whose numbers reached half a million in Malaysia and who were employed in Malaysia's IT sector as well as in the F&B industry. TNCC implied that India may lose the remittances that come from those who were employed in Malaysia should there be retaliatory actions by Malaysia in response to India's possible banning of Malaysia's palm oil (Anon 2019g). TNCC's call for restraint was certainly in consideration of the Indian migrant workers in Malaysia who come mainly from South India. Eventually, India imposed a restriction on imports of refined palm oil from Malaysia in January 2020 (Jadhav 2020; Anon 2020c). Nevertheless, four months later, in May 2020, under a new Malaysian Prime Minister, India resumed imports of palm oil from Malaysia (Jadhav and Thukral 2020). This rapprochement came after Malaysia undertook to increase its imports of sugar and rice from India by nearly 50 percent and 100 percent, respectively (Jadhav and Thukral 2020; Anon 2020b), and after Muhyiddin took over as Malaysia's Prime Minister in March 2020. The Indian High Commissioner to Malaysia was the first top diplomat to be invited by Muhyiddin for a one-on-one discussion after taking the helm (Anon 2020a).

The placatory moves were necessary given the importance of the Indian market to Malaysia. The impact of the restriction imposed by India was quite considerable on Malaysia's palm oil exports. In 2019, Malaysia exported over 18.46 million metric tons (MT) of palm oil to the world, and exports to India stood at the highest with 4.41 million MT. This was followed by China (2.49 million MT) and Pakistan (1.08 million MT). In 2020 (January–August), palm oil exports to India dipped over 67 percent from 3.59 million MT for the same period in 2019 to 1.17 million MT. Owing to the restrictions imposed by India, China became Malaysia's main export market for palm oil for the period of January–August 2020 with exports to China registering at 1.39 million MT, an increase of 32 percent from the corresponding period in

2019. Exports to Pakistan in the same period increased by nearly 7 percent to 751 million MT from 702 million MT from the corresponding period in 2019 (MPOB 2020).

Another bump in India–Malaysia ties in the past occurred in 2003 when Malaysia's police detained 270 Indian IT professionals suspected to have been illegal workers in the country. This saw the High Commissioner of India to Malaysia requesting a formal explanation for the ill-treatment of India's IT professionals, who all had legal working permits. Malaysia's High Commissioner in Delhi was also summoned by India's Minister of External Affairs. Some of the professionals were employed at renowned IT establishments in Malaysia's Multimedia Super Corridor (MSC) in Cyberjaya (Anon 2003b). In essence, the Indian IT professionals were important to Malaysia's growing ICT ecosystem. The MSC was critical in Malaysia's plan to be a global ICT hub. In fact at that time India's Satyam was about to establish its global solutions center with investments of RM2 million at Cyberjaya after a two-year discussion with the Malaysian Government (Anon 2003c). India was reported to have been considering retaliatory economic actions against Malaysia for the incident (Chengappa 2012), but tensions were diffused after Malaysia's Deputy Prime Minister Tun Abdullah Ahmad Badawi apologized for the incident (Anon 2003a).

The Road Ahead

During the post–Cold War period, political personalities have continued to play significant roles in the strengthening of the bilateral ties between Malaysia and India. However, there are also incidents that highlight some of the challenges that such personalities present to the ties between the countries. Perception also has a part in this. Looking from Malaysia's perspective, given the changes that have swept through the Malaysian political scene since 2018, it is now more apparent than before that consistency in the country's policies with regard to India is a sure way of avoiding further crucibles in our bilateral economic relationship. There is a need to be focused on the opportunities, some of which were induced by the Covid-19 predicament, in this bilateral economic partnership.

The Covid-19 crisis has dealt a serious blow to economies all over the world and India is among those most hard hit (International Monetary Fund [IMF] 2020). Nevertheless, in response, India has embarked on a series of reforms to make its economy more resilient in the long run. The *Aatma Nirbhar Bharat Abhiyaan* (Self-Reliant India Movement) campaign by Modi includes reforms to the MSMEs, labor market, industries, and India's vast middle class (IBEF 2020). India's agriculture sector is already seeing unprecedented levels of reforms, and this itself is set to be a boon for the economy, which is heavily dependent on agriculture (Chandra Babu and Dassani 2020; Spindles and Agarwal 2020). In line with these initiatives, India is set to pump in RS110 trillion into a National Pipeline Project for the overall infrastructure development of the country. This is expected to boost the country's infrastructure projects, in the next five years, involving 7,000 projects in various sectors (PM India 2020).

These will bring in many opportunities for further collaborations. The good bilateral working relationships at the various G-2-G as well as B-2-B platforms such as India-Malaysia CEOs' Forum will serve well in identifying the various opportunities that will open up for closer alliances. Mutually beneficial on-going engagements between the business councils and chambers of both countries through the Malaysian Associated Indian Chambers of Commerce and Industry (MAICCI), Malaysia-Indian Business Council (MIBC), ASEAN India-Business Council (AIBC), the Confederation of Indian Industry (CII) and the Federation of Indian Chambers of Commerce and Industry (FICCI) also play a critical role in ensuring that bilateral economic ties evolve according to the challenges of the times. As for the Malaysian construction firms, they have further opportunities to leverage on their existing linkages to participate in the infrastructure development that is expected to sweep across India for years to come. All this has the potential to further boost efforts by Malaysia and India in improving trade facilitation, so that trade between the two countries can be broadened and diversified. The main challenges that have been cited by businesses from both sides for the low utilization of MICECA, for example, are related to the verification procedures that still require further discussions and facilitations by both governments (MITI 2015). This could alleviate India's balance of trade challenge incurred by palm oil imports, which is a commodity that India needs for its domestic consumption and cannot do without in the near future.

CONCLUSION

Since the 1990s economic and commercial relations have been the mainstay of the bilateral partnership between India and Malaysia. Trade and investment collectively over the years have assumed a greater role in promoting our good and cordial relations. Over the last decade and until 2018, exchange of visits from leaders and ministers had taken place almost every year with high-level visits between the leaders of the two countries. The emphasis between the leaders of the two countries has always been on the need to develop a closer partnership to tap the huge unrealized economic potential present between not only Malaysia and India but between ASEAN and India as well. As such, it is important to keep the focus on the opportunities that lie latent between

Malaysia and India, even as both countries attempt to rejuvenate their own economies to face the onslaught of global challenges ahead.

REFERENCES

Abas, Azura. 2019. "Greater Demand for Malaysian Palm Oil from India and China." *New Straits Times*, 14 November. https://www.nst.com.my/news/nation/2019/11/538580/greater-demand-malaysian-palm-oil-india-and-china.

Anon. 2003a. "Badawi Apologises for Ill-Treatment of Indians in Malaysia." *Zeenews,* 21 March. https://zeenews.india.com/news/nation/badawi-apologises-for-illtreatment-of-indians-in-malaysia_87129.html.

———. 2003b. "India Protests at Malaysian Police Raid on IT Workers." *ComputerWeekly.Com*, 10 March. https://www.computerweekly.com/news/2240049837/India-protests-at-Malaysian-police-raid-on-IT-workers.

———. 2003c. "Satyam of India Sets up Centre in Cyberjaya." *The Star,* 29 April. https://www.thestar.com.my/business/business-news/2003/04/29/satyam-of-india-sets-up-centre-in-cyberjaya.

———. 2008. "India, Malaysia to Ink Multi-Million Dollar Railway Deal." *The Economic Times, 13 May.* https://economictimes.indiatimes.com/industry/transportation/railways/india-malaysia-to-ink-multi-million-dollar-railway-deal/articleshow/3036247.cms?utm_source=contentofinterest&utm_medium=text&utm_campaign=cppst.

———. 2010. "India, Malaysia Sign CECA; Set USD 15 Bn Trade Target by 2015." *The Indian Express,* 27 October. http://archive.indianexpress.com/news/india-malaysia-sign-ceca--set-usd-15-bn-trade-target-by-2015/703229/.

———. 2011a. "India and Malaysia Sign MoU for Highway Development." India Infoline News Service, 22 December. https://www.indiainfoline.com/article/news-top-story/india-and-malaysia-sign-mou-for-highway-development-113101800805_1.html.

———. 2011b. "Malaysia to Collaborate with India on Infrastructure." *The Economic Times,* 7 January. https://economictimes.indiatimes.com/news/economy/infrastructure/malaysia-to-collaborate-with-india-on-infrastructure/articleshow/7236107.cms?utm_source=contentofinterest&utm_medium=text&utm_campaign=cppst.

———. 2011c. "Samy Vellu Begins Special Envoy Duties." *The Star,* 3 January. https://www.thestar.com.my/news/nation/2011/01/03/samy-vellu-begins-special-envoy-duties.

———. 2017a. "Indian Railways to Offer 20 Stations to Malaysia for Redevelopment." *The Economic Times,* 7 July. https://economictimes.indiatimes.com/industry/transportation/railways/indian-railways-to-offer-20-stations-to-malaysia-for-redevelopment/articleshow/59031452.cms?utm_source=contentofinterest&utm_medium=text&utm_campaign=cppst.

———. 2017b. "Malaysia Wants to Raise Ties with India to New Heights: PM Najib Abdul Razak." *The Indian Express*, 1 April. https://indianexpress.com/article/india

/malaysia-wants-to-raise-ties-with-india-to-new-heights-pm-najib-abdul-razak
-4595695/.

———. 2018. "Evolution of the Malaysian Economy." *The Edge Markets*, 17 September.   https://www.theedgemarkets.com/article/evolution-malaysian
-economy.

———. 2019a. "'Desist from Making Such Remarks': MEA on Malaysian PM's Kashmir Comment." *The Indian Express*, 4 October. https://indianexpress
.com/article/india/jammu-and-kashmir-unga-malaysia-turkey-mea-raveesh-kumar
-6053583/.

———. 2019b. "Dr M's Full Speech Text at the 74th UNGA." *NST Malaysia*, 28 September. https://www.nst.com.my/news/nation/2019/09/525269/dr-ms-full
-speech-text-74th-unga.

———. 2019c. "India Trade Body Tells Members Not to Import Malaysian Palm Oil in Nationalistic Protest." *The Star*, 21 October. https://www.thestar.com.my/news/
nation/2019/10/21/india-trade-body-tells-members-not-to-import-malaysian-palm
-oil-in-nationalistic-protest.

———. 2019d. "Industry, Traders & Farmers Welcome India's Decision to Not Sign RCEP." *The Economic Times*, 5 November. https://retail.economictimes.indiatimes
.com/news/industry/industry-traders-farmers-welcome-indias-decision-to-not-sign
-rcep/71915784.

———. 2019e. "Malaysia Scrambling to Manage India Palm Oil Boycott Call." *New Straits Times*, 27 October. https://www.nst.com.my/news/nation/2019/10/533638/
malaysia-scrambling-manage-india-palm-oil-boycott-call.

———. 2019f. "MEA Summons Malaysian Diplomat Over PM Mahathir's Criticism of Citizenship Law." *The Wire*, 22 December. New Delhi. https://thewire.in
/diplomacy/mea-summons-malaysian-diplomat-over-pm-mahathirs-criticism-of
-citizenship-law.

———. 2019g. "New Twist to Malaysia-India Palm Oil Issue." *The Star*, 23 October. https://www.thestar.com.my/business/business-news/2019/10/23/new-twist-to
-malaysia-india-palm-oil-issue#:~:text=KUALA LUMPUR%3A The Malaysia-
India,palm oil imports from Malaysia.

———. 2020a. "Exclusive: Malaysia to Buy More Sugar from India to Help Resolve Palm Oil Spat— Sources." *Business Insider*, 23 January. https://www
.businessinsider.com/exclusive-malaysia-to-buy-more-sugar-from-india-to-help
-resolve-palm-oil-spat-sources-2020-1.

———. 2020b. "Malaysia Signs Record Rice Import Deal with India." *The Star*, 17 May. https://www.thestar.com.my/news/regional/2020/05/17/exporters-malaysia
-signs-record-rice-import-deal-with-india.

———. 2020c. "Malaysian Palm Oil Price Surges as India Restricts Refined Palm Oil Imports." *The Star*, 10 January. https://www.thestar.com.my/business/business
-news/2020/01/10/malaysian-palm-oil-price-surges-as-india-restricts-refined-palm
-oil-imports.

———. 2020d. "Muhyiddin to Clear Mahathir's 'Mess' with India." *The Capital Post*, 18 April. https://www.capitalpost.com.my/2020/04/17/muhyiddin-to-clear
-mahathirs-mess-with-india/.

ASEAN. 1967. "The ASEAN Declaration (Bangkok Declaration) Bangkok, 8 August 1967." *About ASEAN*. https://asean.org/the-asean-declaration-bangkok-declaration-bangkok-8-august-1967/.

———. 2019a. "Joint Leaders' Statement on RCEP, 4 November." *Statements*. https://doi.org/10.1017/CBO9781107415324.004.

———. 2019b. "Joint Media Statement: The Sixteenth AEM-India Consultations, 10 September 2019, Bangkok, Thailand." *ASEAN Secretariat*. 2019. https://asean.org/storage/2019/09/AEM-India-16-JMS-FINAL.pdf.

Basu Das, Sanchita. 2018. "ASEAN-India Economic Relations: Low Base, Large Potential." *ISEAS Perspective*, no. 68: 1–12.

Birdsall, Nancy M., Jose Edgardo L. Campos, Chang-Shik Kim, W. Max Corden, John Page, Richard Sabor, and Joseph E Stiglitz. 1993. *The East Asian Miracle: Economic Growth and Public Policy*. Edited by Lawrence MacDonald. Washington, DC: World Bank Group. http://documents.worldbank.org/curated/en/975081468244550798/Main-report.

Blank, Jonah, Jennifer D. P. Moroney, Angel Rabasa, and Bonny Lin. 2015. "What Is India's Strategy Toward Southeast Asia?" In *Look East, Cross Black Waters: India's Interest in Southeast Asia*, 22–78.

Chandra Babu, Suresh, and Vaishali Dassani. 2020. "COVID-19-Induced Policy Reforms in India: Overcoming Implementation Challenges." *Inter Press Service*, 22 October. http://www.ipsnews.net/2020/07/covid-19-induced-policy-reforms-india-overcoming-implementation-challenges/.

Chengappa, Raj. 2012. "Indian IT Professionals Harassed in Malaysia, India Plans Economic Retaliatory Measures." *India Today*, 2 July. https://www.indiatoday.in/magazine/diplomacy/story/20030324-indian-it-professionals-harassed-in-malaysia-enraged-india-plans-economic-retaliatory-measures-793287-2003-03-24.

CIDB Malaysia. 2015. "Journey of Time 20 Years." Construction Industry Development Board Malaysia. 2015. https://www.cidb.gov.my/sites/default/files/2020-12/Journey of Time 20 Years.pdf.

Department of Statistics Malaysia. 2021. "Trade Performance (Various Years)." *Malaysia's Trade Performance: MATRADE*. http://www.matrade.gov.my/en/malaysian-exporters/services-for-exporters/trade-market-information/trade-statistics.

IBEF. 2020. "Self-Reliant India Movement: An Opportunity." *India Brand Equity Foundation*, 20 May. https://www.ibef.org/blogs/self-reliant-india-movement-an-opportunity.

International Monetary Fund (IMF). 2020. "World Economic Outlook Update." June. https://www.imf.org/en/Publications/WEO/Issues/2020/06/24/WEOUpdateJune2020.

Jadhav, Rajendra. 2020. "UPDATE 1—India Restricts Refined Palm Oil Imports after Malaysia's Criticism of Modi." *Reuters*, 8 January. https://www.reuters.com/article/india-palmoil-imports-idUSL4N29D300.

Jadhav, Rajendra, and Naveen Thukral. 2020. "Exclusive: India Resumes Purchases of Malaysian Palm Oil—Traders." *Reuters*, 19 May. https://www.reuters.com/article/us-india-malaysia-palmoil-exclusive-idUSKBN22V0QM.

Jha, Kundan. 2020. "India, Indonesia Negotiating Economic Cooperation Agreement." *The Sunday Guardian,* 25 January. https://www.sundayguardianlive.com/news/ india-indonesia-negotiating-economic-cooperation-agreement.

Kachiar, Yatharth. 2020. "Will a New Government in Malaysia Reset India Ties?" *The Diplomat,* 20 April. https://thediplomat.com/2020/04/will-a-new-government -in-malaysia-reset-india-ties/.

MEA. 2019a. "Factually Inaccurate Remarks by Prime Minister of Malaysia on CAA." Press Release, 20 December. https://www.mea.gov.in/press-releases.htm ?dtl/32230/Factually_Inaccurate_Remarks_by_Prime_Minister_of_Malaysia_on _CAA.

———. 2019b. "Transcript of Media Briefing by Secretary (East) during PM's Visit to Thailand (November 04, 2019)." Media Briefings. https://mea.gov.in/ media-briefings.htm?dtl/32007/Transcript_of_Media_Briefing_by_Secretary_East _during_PMs_visit_to_Thailand_November_04_2019.

———. 2020a. "Brief on India-Malaysia Bilateral Relations." February. https://mea .gov.in/Portal/ForeignRelation/Unclassified_bilataeral_brief_on_India-Malaysia _relations_24_Sep_2019.pdf.

———. 2020b. "Brief on India-Malaysia Bilateral Relations." *Foreign Relations,* 3 February. https://mea.gov.in/foreign-relations.htm.

———. 2020c. "India-Indonesia Bilateral Brief." Bilateral Brief. https://mea.gov.in/ Portal/ForeignRelation/INDIA_INDONESIA__2019.pdf.

MIDA. 2010. "India Encourages Malaysian Participation in Its Road Projects." *Cross Border News MIDA,* 7 January. https://www.mida.gov.my/home/617/news/india -encourages-malaysian-participation-in-its-road-projects-/.

———. 2019. "Indian Investors to Capitalise on Business Opportunities in Malaysia." *MIDA in the News,* 14 February. https://www.mida.gov.my/home/8131 /news/indian-investors-to-capitalise-on-business-opportunities-in-malaysia/.

MITI. 2011. "Malaysia International Trade and Industry Report 2010: Chapter 1: World Economic, Trade and Investment Developments." Kuala Lumpur. https:// www.miti.gov.my/miti/resources/auto download images/55555e15dc816.pdf.

———. 2015. "Press Release: Malaysia Keen to Invest for Successful Make in India Initiative: Malaysian Trade and Industry Minister Dato' Sri Mustapa Bin Mohamed."

———. 2017. "Media Release: Malaysia-India Business Forum Held In Conjunction With The Official Visit Of Yab Prime Minister To Republic Of India 3 April 2017, Taj Palace Hotel, New Delhi." https://www.miti.gov.my/miti/resources/Media _Release_-_Malaysia-India_Business_Forum_Held_In_Conjunction_With_The _Official_Visit_Of_YAB_Prime_Minister_To_Republic_Of_India_3_April_2017 ,_Taj_Palace_Hotel,_New_Delhi.pdf.

———. 2020. "Questions on Malaysia-India CECA (MICECA)." Free Trade Agreements. 2020. https://www.miti.gov.my/index.php/pages/view/2202.

MOF. 2020. "The Economic Survey 2019–20, Volume 2, Services Sector." *Ministry of Finance India.* https://www.indiabudget.gov.in/economicsurvey/doc/vol2chapter/ echap09_vol2.pdf.

MPOB. 2020. "Monthly Palm Oil Trade Statistics: January–December 2019 & January–August 2020." MPOC Statistics. http://mpoc.org.my/monthly-palm-oil -trade-statistics/.

Murphy, Stephen A. 2018. "Revisiting the Bujang Valley: A Southeast Asian Entrepôt Complex on the Maritime Trade Route." *Journal of the Royal Asiatic Society* 28 (2): 355–89.

National Economic Advisory Council Malaysia. 2010. "Where Are We?" In *New Economic Model For Malaysia Part 1*, 1st ed., 41–45. Kuala Lumpur: Percetakan Nasional Malaysia Berhad. https://www.epu.gov.my/sites/default/files/2020-02/ nem.pdf.

Nehru, Vikram. 2011. "Southeast Asia: Crouching Tiger or Hidden Dragon?" *Carnegie Endowment For International Peace,* 7 July. https://carnegieendowment .org/2011/07/07/southeast-asia-crouching-tiger-or-hidden-dragon-pub-44964.

Ong, Justin. 2018. "Report: Putrajaya Axing Special Envoys, Advisers." *The Malay Mail,* 2 July. https://www.malaymail.com/news/malaysia/2018/07/02/report -putrajaya-axing-special-envoys-advisers/1647827.

PM India. 2020. "PM's Address to the Nation from the Ramparts of the Red Fort." News Updates, 15 August. https://www.pmindia.gov.in/en/news_updates/pms -address-to-the-nation-from-the-ramparts-of-the-red-fort/?comment=disable.

Saraswat, V. K., Prachi Priya, and Aniruddha Ghosh. 2018. "A Note on Free Trade Agreements and Their Costs." *National Institution for Transforming India (NITI Aayog).* https://niti.gov.in/writereaddata/files/document_publication/FTA-NITI -FINAL.pdf.

Shivkumar, C. 2013. "Nellore Bypass Job Goes To Indo-Malaysia Consortium." *Business Standard,* 26 February. https://www.business-standard.com/article/ specials/nellore-bypass-job-goes-to-indo-malaysia-consortium-198022601047_1 .html.

Singh, Amit. 2009. "India's Diaspora Policy: A Case Study of Indians in Malaysia." Ph.D. Thesis. Jawaharlal Nehru University.

Spindles, Bill, and Vibhuti Agarwal. 2020. "India Turns to Economic Overhaul as Growth Prospects Slide Amid Coronavirus." *Wall Street Journal, 13 October*. https: //www.wsj.com/articles/india-turns-to-economic-overhaul-as-growth-prospects -slide-amid-coronavirus-11602586802.

Chapter 3

Strengthening Malaysia–India People-to-People (P2P) Connectivity Through Tourism

Suseela Devi Chandran

INTRODUCTION

The "Visit Truly Asia Malaysia 2020" campaign is the latest campaign launched by the Malaysian government in the series of Visit Malaysia campaigns. It was launched in line with the Malaysia Tourism Transformation Plan goals of welcoming a total 30 million tourists to Malaysia and registering RM 100 billion in tourist receipts by the year 2020. The goal of Visit Malaysia 2020 is to unite all industry players to achieving this common goal, whilst simultaneously attracting tourists from all over the globe to experience first-hand the warm hospitality and numerous tourist attractions Malaysia is well known for. The first Visit Malaysia Year (VMY) campaign was launched in 1990 to promote tourism in the country. The campaign was a huge success with Malaysia charting 7.4 million tourist arrivals compared to 4.8 million in 1989. Prior to 1990, the revenue from tourism also increased from the range of RM 1 billion to RM 2 billion. The success of VMY 1990 (RM 4.5 billion) spurred the government to launch the second VMY in 1994. By then, in 1994 the revenue from tourism increased significantly (RM 8.3 billion) (http://www.tourism.gov.my). Incidentally, in 2004, MOCAT was restructured to facilitate the establishment of a separate ministry responsible solely for matters related to tourism (i.e., the Ministry of Tourism [MOT]).

This reflected Malaysia's government determination to intensify efforts to promote tourism as it has become one of the major revenue earners for the country. Tourism is the third biggest contributor to Malaysia's GDP, after manufacturing and commodities. In 2018, this sector contributed around 5.9 percent to the total GDP. In recent years, the tourism industry in Southeast Asia has experienced significant growth, and Malaysia is keen to capitalize on this trend. Currently, the ministry has been recognized to become the Ministry of Tourism and Culture (MOTAC) and is reputed to be the second largest foreign exchange earner next to the manufacturing sector for the country. The third VMY was launched in 2007 in conjunction with Malaysia's 50th Independence Anniversary. In 2014, Malaysia celebrated its fourth Visit Malaysia Year with the theme "Celebrating 1Malaysia Truly Asia" to reflect the diversity in unity of the nation (see http://www.vmy2014 .com/about-vmy2014/history-of-visit-malaysia-year). Hence, it is palpable that the tourism industry has progressed significantly over the years, and this development is aided by the government's emphasis on achieving the following: i. generating foreign exchange earnings, ii. increasing employment in the industry, iii. fostering regional/rural development, iv. diversifying the country's economic base, v. the promotion of the country's cultural diversity, and vi. promoting tourism industry abroad (Review of National Tourism Policy Main Report, Ministry of Tourism Malaysia 2004, 5).

Table 3.1 illustrates the contributions of the tourism industry to Malaysia from 2007–2018. As indicated in Table 3.1, revenue growth from tourism industry has been generally consistent, albeit with some fluctuations in 2008. The decline is attributable to the global recession which crippled the economies of most Southeast Asian countries. However, since then, there has been a steady growth in tourism. The year 2018 recorded the highest revenue

Table 3.1: Malaysia tourism revenue growth

Year	Revenue (RM Billion)	Arrivals (Million)
2007	53.4	20.97
2008	49.6	22.05
2009	53.4	23.65
2010	56.5	24.58
2011	58.3	24.71
2012	60.6	25.03
2013	65.4	25.72
2014	72.0	27.44
2015	69.1	25.72
2016	82.1	26.76
2017	82.1	25.95
2018	84.1	25.83

Source: https://www.tourism.gov.my/statistics

(RM 84.1 billion), while the highest arrivals were in 2014 (27.44 million tourists). For the year 2018, 25.83 million tourists arrived in Malaysia, compared with the target of 26.4 million, even though year-on-year (y-o-y) this was a 0.4 percent decline from the 2017 figure of 25.95 million (http://www.tourism.gov.my).

From the grand total of 25.83 million tourists to Malaysia, Singapore recorded the highest tourist arrivals in 2018 with 10.62 million arrivals. Aside from Singapore, other top tourist arrivals in 2018 were from Indonesia (3.28 million), China (2.94 million), Thailand (1.91 million), Brunei (1.38 million), South Korea (616,783), India (600,311), the Philippines (396,062), Japan (394,540) and Taiwan (383,922). The top 10 markets for international inbound tourist are shown in Table 3.2.

The tourism industry's contribution to economic development has been made possible through the development and improvement of tourism prod-

Table 3.2: Top 10 tourist arrivals by country of nationality, 2018

No	Country	Number of Tourist Arrivals (Million)
1.	Singapore	10.62
2.	Indonesia	3.28
3.	China (including Hong Kong and Macau)	2.94
4.	Thailand	1.91
5.	Brunei	1.38
6.	South Korea	0.616
7.	India	0.600
8.	Philippines	0.396
9.	Japan	0.394
10.	Taiwan	0.383

Source: Tourism Malaysia (2020)

ucts over the last three decades to cater to the growing demands of a wide range of local, regional and international tourists. The tourism industry in Malaysia is an important foreign exchange earner, contributing to economic growth, attracting investments and providing employment.

One of the goals the Malaysian government has placed in the tourism industry is resolute in its endeavour to promote an understanding of the various cultures and lifestyles of the multiethnic population of Malaysia, and to create awareness and enhance Malaysia's image abroad (Review of National Tourism Policy, Policy Report, Ministry of Tourism Malaysia 2004, 4). Over the years, the taglines used by the tourism industry to sculpt and portray the image of Malaysia have evolved from "Beautiful Malaysia" to "Only Malaysia," followed by "Fascinating Malaysia" and "Malaysia Truly Asia."

Through efforts to expand the tourist attractions, CNN Travel announced Malaysia as one of the 17 must-visit destinations in 2019 based on the total of 25.83 million tourists who visited Malaysia in 2018.

MALAYSIA–INDIA TOURISM

India has emerged as one of the biggest and most important outbound travel markets in the world. A report from Amadeus-Frost & Sullivan stated that over the past five years, outbound travel from India has more than doubled. India has been an important country to Malaysia in terms of contribution to Malaysia's tourism industry. India has been consistently among the top 10 nations with regard to the volume of tourists.

The role of the Malaysian government in increasing and attracting Indian tourists is apparent. The presence of three overseas Tourism Malaysia representative offices in India, namely in New Delhi, Mumbai, and Chennai, signifies the importance attached to the Indian market by Malaysia. According to the Malaysian Tourism officer in New Delhi, each representative in New Delhi, Mumbai and Chennai looks after a designated region of India. For example, the Tourism Malaysia office in New Delhi takes care of the states in the northern region of India such as Rajasthan, Orissa, Haryana, Punjab and others. Whereas Tourism Malaysia Mumbai covers the central states of India, and Tourism Malaysia Chennai is responsible for the southern states of India, namely Tamil Nadu, Kerala, and Karnataka. The role of tourism representatives in India is not confined only to do marketing and promotion but also to establish a good bilateral relation with the host country, India, and network closely with the Indian government, travel agents and with the private sectors.

Malaysia was one of the late entrants to establish a tourism office in India, but Malaysia has realized that India is a dynamic and vibrant market and it is important to tap the market well. India remains the sixth top tourist generating market to Malaysia.

According to MOTAC, the Indian tourist market has been a specific target for the last few years and the Malaysian government has been conducting aggressive campaigns to attract more Indian tourists. Ministry of Tourism Malaysia undertakes annual sales missions to India covering cities such as Bangalore, Mumbai and New Delhi. The missions involve programmes such as travel mart sessions, press conferences, dialogues, interviews by the local media, dinner functions, courtesy calls to the High Commissioner and Consul General of Malaysia and sales pitches to tour operators in the cities. The objective of the mission is to showcase Malaysia's commitment to collaborate with travel agencies, airlines and overseas media to promote Malaysia as a top tourist destination.

Given the overall growth in the total numbers of tourist arrivals from India to Malaysia, Malaysia is expected to be the first Asian country to be able to tap the large tourist market in India. The ringgit's depreciation would also benefit tourists visiting Malaysia, which is also viewed as a budget destination. Malaysia has wide options to attract tourists from India, mainly luxury adventure, meetings, weddings, shopping, conventions, and exhibitions.

In general, Malaysia's main attraction from India is among the individual families, especially the higher-end group, young couples and the business community. Also, another source of attraction lies in golfing activities, or popularly known as *golf tourism*. Around 80 percent of golf destinations for Indian holiday makers are confined to Southeast Asia. An estimated 714,405 rounds of golf were played by foreign visitors in 2012. Malaysia's popularity as a golf destination among the Indian tourists has grown over the years. With around 207 golf courses, ranging from short 9-hole courses to 54-hole complexes, Malaysia is attracting lot of Indian golfers (see http://corporate .tourism.gov.my/mediacentre.asp?page=feature_malaysia&subpage=archive &news_id=101).

According to the Tourism Malaysia (India) Director, the greens fees for the golf courses in Malaysia are among the lowest in Asia. Moreover, Malaysia's golf courses offer challenging fairways amidst spectacular sights and world-class facilities and amenities. This has helped Malaysia in attracting Indian tourists, especially the golfers. Capitalizing on the increasing interest of the Indian tourists towards Malaysia, the government has also introduced new tourism packages. In 2009, the Malaysian government introduced "A-One Malaysia, Endless Experience." This package includes a holiday package of Rps 17,000 for travel from anywhere in India to Kuala Lumpur. The four-day/three-night package includes return airfare and accommodations. Tourism Malaysia offers interesting flexible packages (such as choosing the destination, accommodations and travel assistance) to meet the demands of Indian tourists.

Another area of attraction among the Indian tourists is *medical/health tourism*. Medical tourism is a new form of a niche tourism market which has been rapidly expanding in recent years. Many scholars like Goodrich and Goodrich (1987), Laws (1996), Connell (2006) in Dawn & Pal (2011) described medical tourism as an activity whereby people travel to overseas countries to obtain healthcare services and facilities such as medical, dental, and surgical care whilst having the opportunity to visit the tourist spots of that country. Moreover, Bookman & Bookman (2007) in Dawn & Pal (2011) have defined medical tourism as travel with the aim of improving one's health, and also as an economic activity that entails trade in services and represents two sectors, which are tourism and medicine.

One interesting phenomena in medical tourism is that, based on the available information gathered, a substantial number of patients travel to developing nations for healthcare treatment. The primary reason to seek medical services in less developed countries is the attractively low cost (Horowitz et al. 2007, 35). Another reason is because developing countries can provide healthcare services inexpensively, which is directly related to the nation's economic status. Indeed, the prices charged for medical care in a destination country generally correlate with that nation's per capita gross domestic product. Among the countries that are approached for medical treatment are India and Thailand. Other Asian countries that are currently promoting medical tourism, besides India and Thailand, are Malaysia, Singapore, and South Korea.

In the last few years, Malaysia has garnered high repute in medical tourism and is seen as one of the ideal destinations for healthcare needs. As healthcare in Malaysia is regulated by the Ministry of Health, the treatment is perceived as reliable, safe and effective and with the added benefit of comfortable surroundings with ease of access and at affordable prices. Although India itself is one of the countries promoting medical tourism, this has not deterred the Indians from seeking out other developing countries like Malaysia for medical treatments.

According to a Tourism Malaysia representative in New Delhi, many Indians in India perceive Malaysia's medical/health services as quality, trustworthy and credible. Ther latest statistics indicate that Indonesian tourists who came to Malaysia for medical/health assistance logged the highest number, followed by India, Japan, United Kingdom, Iran, Nepal and Bangladesh. For the last five years, there were about 20,000 Indian tourists who sought medical treatment and healthcare facilities in Malaysia. The Malaysian government believes that there are many factors, such as effective marketing strategy, timely response to the needs of tourists, cost-effective treatments, quality treatment and care, availability of latest medicines at affordable rates, state-of-the-art technology, and environment friendly facilities—all of which have contributed to the increase of health tourism.

The National Heart Institute (IJN) is trying to attract Indian patients by offering advanced healthcare at a fraction of the price they pay at hospitals in the United States and Europe. According to the Medical Tourism Manager in IJN, Malaysia hospitals do not only offer latest medical technology, but the total environment for treatment. Moreover, for the first time, the Malaysian hospital was named as the top hospital for medical tourists in the annual ranking by the Medical Travel Quality Alliance (MTQUA) for the year 2017. As such, with top-notch medical services providing reliable, safe and effective treatments in comfortable surroundings with ease of access and affordable prices, Malaysia has certainly become a leading choice for foreign patients seeking healthcare treatments abroad. Hence, it is evident that many patients head towards Malaysia for medical treatments. Another key factor that makes Malaysia the preferred destination for medical tourism is the cost difference compared to other countries such as Thailand, India, Singapore and South Korea.

In general, there are many factors that contribute to the increased interest in Malaysia for medical treatment. First, Malaysia is amongst one of the few countries within the region where medical tourism is promoted by the government. This official support provides medical tourists the assurance on quality care, regulations, safety standards and the governing laws within this industry. Second, Malaysian healthcare offers specialties in various medical disciplines and medical practices that are on par with some of the developed countries, incorporating both sophistication as well as international expertise. Thirdly, medical treatments in Malaysia are carried out in state-of-the-art facilities that have been furnished to meet international standards. Hence, the high quality in medical treatments is thus maintained at the technology as well as at the professional level. And finally, healthcare facilities in Malaysia are complemented by equally proficient doctors and nurses. The biggest advantage is perhaps the fact that the faculties of the hospitals are English speaking.

Besides medical/health tourism, Malaysia is also a well-known honeymoon/wedding destination for Indian couples. For the last few years, wedding destinations in Malaysia have captured Indians' attention and Malaysia is keenly aware of the great potential the industry can bring to its tourism business. Last year, Tourism Malaysia invited six of India's top wedding planners from Mumbai, Chennai and Delhi to see what Malaysia could offer as a wedding destination for their clients. Malaysia has a huge tourist appeal due to its scenic locations, rich culture, heritage and exotic cuisine. The towering skyscrapers of contemporary Kuala Lumpur to the verdant tea plantations and varied forms of nature are among the attractions Indians seek to either spend their honeymoons or conduct their weddings here. Among the favorite locations among the Indians are Langkawi and Sabah. Furthermore, Malaysia has quite a few themes to offer when it comes to weddings—such as city weddings, resort weddings, beach weddings and hillside weddings. With a coastline of almost 5,000 kilometers in the Peninsula and Borneo, beach weddings are one of the favorite themes often booked by Indian families. Another contributing factor that attracts the Indian market to conduct weddings here is the cultural factor. The cultural factor provides the perfect setting for Indian couples to hold their weddings. Places of worship such as temples, churches and gurdwaras, as well as availability of vegetarian restaurants and professional vendors, ensure organizing an Indian destination wedding in Malaysia is very convenient to the families of the bride and groom.

Another programme under Tourism Malaysia that attracts Indian tourists is "Malaysia My Second Home" (MM2H). This programme was launched by the government to welcome foreigners to reside or retire in Malaysia. They are provided with a 10-year Social Visit Pass and Multiple Entry visa which could be continuously renewed. Under this programme various privileges and benefits are offered, and it is considered one of the most attractive long-term-stay visa programmes across Asia. This programme has attracted more than 23,000 participants from different countries. The Indian nationals have participated in the MM2H programme since it was initiated. Although India is listed as one of the top 10 countries, nevertheless there has not been much interest among the Indians in this programme compared to other nations. This has encouraged Tourism Malaysia to further promote this programme to the people of India extensively whenever road shows are carried out.

In addition, another factor that contributes to the increase in tourism is the air connectivity. The extraordinary growth in international travel over the last decades is seen as very much due to advances in air transport and the rise of the middle-class group. The establishment of various airline companies, especially the low-cost airlines such as Air Asia Bhd (Malaysia), has definitely increased the connectivity of people from Malaysia and India. Following a bilateral agreement in 2007 between Malaysia and India, it has progressively increased its seat capacity to six major destinations in India, included a provision for multiple destinations, and designated any number of airlines to operate on the India–Malaysia routes. Currently, Malaysia has eight international airports, and efforts are on-going to improve efficiency and performance at the Kuala Lumpur International Airport (KLIA), with a view of developing KLIA into a regional hub. The main national carrier is Malaysia Airlines (MAS), with other local airlines such as Air Asia flying regional and local routes. Furthermore, the bilateral entitlements for operation of scheduled air services between India and Malaysia have been liberalized/increased under the ASEAN offer. Under this deal, the designated airlines of Malaysia can operate a daily flight to each of the four metropolitan cities of Delhi, Mumbai, Chennai and Kolkata and have unlimited access to 18 tourist destinations in India via Amritsar, Ahmedabad, Calicut, Cochin, Trivandrum, Goa, Gaya, Varanasi, Lucknow, Trichy, Jaipur, Port Blair, Guwahati, Patna, Bhubaneshwar, Aurangabad, Khajuraho and Vizag. Accessibility between the two countries is also gradually increasing. There are 237 weekly flights from India to Malaysia covering 14 Indian cities.

GLOBALIZATION AND TOURISM IN
MALAYSIA–INDIA RELATIONS

The socio-cultural dimension had spurred the efforts in enhancing people-to-people relations. Interactions between the people of the two countries in areas such as tourism, education, culture, entertainment, and Indian diaspora are undeniably pertinent factors that have contributed to the enhancement of the bilateral relations between the two countries. However, as Moses (2012) highlighted, the Malaysian perspective on India has generally derived from the Indian diaspora present in that country (Malaysia). It generally portrays a partial image of India represented only by a group of IT expatriates, professionals and unskilled workers. This perspective on India needs to be changed in Malaysia. India is more than IT experts and a provider of skilled and unskilled labourers. Similarly, India too needs to explore the real socio-cultural aspect of Malaysia. Not all Indians understand Malaysia's culture and not all Malaysians understand the diversity of India. Thus, it is apparent that there is an information divide between both states, and it is necessary to eliminate if not reduce this void. Based on collated data derived from the informants on the socio-cultural dimension (Table 3.3), there is ample room for improvement, especially in terms of improving perceptions and deepening knowledge of each other.

Table 3.3: Socio-cultural respondents

INFORMANTS	ROLE OF STATE		ROLE OF NON-STATE ACTORS#		CONTRIBUTING FACTORS		CHALLENGES
	Facilitator	Primary	Facilitator	External*	Internal**	Perception	Lack of Knowledge
SCR1	√				-	-	√
SCR2	√				√	√	√
SCR3	√				√		√
SCR4	√					√	√
SCR5	√				√	√	
SCR6	√					√	√
SCR7		√		√	√	√	√
SCR8	√				√	√	
SCR9		√		√	√		√

SCR: Socio-cultural respondents (these includes officers from Ministry of Tourism, High Commission of Malaysia in New Delhi, Government Link Companies and Private companies).

#Non-state actors refer to MNC, TNC, NGO, and Civilians/People-to-people.

*External factors in the context of this research refers to post–Cold War geostrategic environment and globalization.

**Internal factors in the context of this research refer to national policies, leadership, and interest.

It is imperative that, at the ground level, initiatives are implemented to ensure basic understanding of each country is achieved. This will set in motion the transformation that will create a broader platform for substantive engagements and dilute misunderstandings between the both countries. The Malaysian government realizes that there should be greater engagement between both nations. One of the efforts taken by the Malaysian government is through Tourism Malaysia. Tourism Malaysia, through its "Malaysia Mega Familiarization" programme (MEGA FAM), is a signature programme for Tourism Malaysia since its inception in 2000. This programme continues to be popular and important in supporting the promotion and branding of Malaysia as a leading tourism destination in the world (Laporan Tahunan 2012, Tourism Malaysia, 81). In 2012, a total of 1,084 foreign guests participated in the MEGA FAM, mainly media representatives, corporate guests and officials. These participants were invited to witness some of the major events in Malaysia such as the Formula 1 Grand Prix, Malaysia International Shoe Festival, Fabulous Food 1Malaysia and 1Malaysia Year-End Sale, among others. Their experiences will be then covered as an international tourism documentary and later developed into new tour packages. This MEGA FAM programme has been successful for Malaysia and the commercial value generated amounted RM 64.1 million in 2012. This was achieved through articles published in foreign print and electronic media (Laporan Tahunan 2012, Tourism Malaysia, 83). Hence, it is evident that Malaysia is not only making efforts to promote through tourism, but also to change the perception of Malaysia amongst the Indians.

Furthermore, globalization has facilitated the increase in tourism through connectivity. Globalization provides easy access to travel due to benefits derived from economies of scale and wide dissemination of information on tourism. While tourism has long been recognized as a source of economic growth, embracing globalization has also geared up an exponential growth in the country's tourism industry. According to the Review of the National Tourism Policy (Executive Summary-Main Report, Ministry of Tourism Malaysia 2004, 4), the key impacts of globalization on the tourism industry are:

- Creation of jobs and increase in investments and increased mobility as people travel for work and leisure
- Leakage in foreign exchange earnings due to greater foreign ownership of local businesses and through greater foreign ownership resulting in higher franchise, licensing, distribution and management fees
- Movement towards a knowledge-based economy whereby emphasis is given to integration and innovation

- Breakdown in cultural borders facilitated by communications and transportation and birth of global culture
- Creation of transnational corporations (TNC) to cater to certain niche areas and reach out to the global markets
- Businesses operating on global strategies and global market presence such as travel agency network and financial services
- Electronic online distribution and trade
- Use of technology to distribute information
- Stimulating the economy and raising standard of living, but this can create social inequality
- Structural changes in the airline industry such as lower domestic and international fares and the existence of charter companies, which increased the accessibility to tourist destinations and general discounts on scheduled airlines.

India opened its economy through globalization and liberalization since 1991, resulting in growth in the tourism sector with spill-over effects in the overall economy. India's economic reforms have elevated the importance of tourism, which is projected as an engine of growth, an instrument for elimination of poverty, a mechanism for solving unemployment woes, and a media for venturing into green fields of activity. New opportunities are being tapped to promote eco-tourism, adventure holidays, rural homestays, wildlife recreation, and healthcare and herbal treatments, including medical tourism. India has liberalized its medical sector to allow the voluntary and private practitioners to offer healthcare and medical treatments to foreign tourists and other citizens. Currently, medical tourism in India includes advanced and life-saving healthcare services like open transplants, cardiovascular surgery, eye treatment, knee/hip procedures, different cosmetic surgeries and alternate systems of medicine. In addition to existence of modern medicines, indigenous or traditional medical practices such as Ayurveda, Siddha, Unani, Naturopathy, and Yoga are well known among foreigners and tourists (Dawn & Pal 2011, 189–190). All these traditional as well as modern healthcare systems are attracting international patients and generating tourism flows.

Malaysia considers India as one of the potential countries for growth of Malaysian tourism. From a mere 30,000 visitors in 1998, the number has gone up sizably to 550,000 in 2008 and 691,271 in 2012. Although India accounts for only 3 percent of total tourist flows into Malaysia, it exhibits a steady rise in numbers every year. With the strong promotional activities by Tourism Malaysia, one could foresee the growth in the tourism industry. Specifically, Tourism Malaysia has launched various programmes to attract tourists from India. Among these initiatives are:

i. Providing a platform known as Sales Mission to major cities in India as well as secondary cities (second-tier city), especially those with direct flights to Malaysia. The objective of this is to strengthen networking between the tourism operators in the two countries. In addition, collaborate with the local agency to increase the number of tourist arrivals from India through the operation of charter flights to Malaysia.

ii. Participating in major tourism fairs in India along with Malaysian tourism industry players and airlines to promote and sell travel packages to Malaysia. Among the major exhibitions are South Asia Travel and Trade Exhibition (SATTE), Sales Mission to South Asia, Make it Malaysia India, and India International Travel Mart.

iii. Organizing promotional programmes targeted directly to consumers, such as the Malaysia Travel Fair, which is dedicated to captivate the interests of Malaysian tourists and sell travel packages to the tourists in the country.

iv. Increasing efforts to promote Malaysia through internet and social media as well as through a variety of media for advertising campaigns in print and electronic media.

v. Enhancing the cooperative network through the Mega Familiarization (MEGA FAM) program, under which journalists are brought to witness tourism-related events organized by the Tourism Ministry in Malaysia, as well as to visit the major tourist destinations. The MEGA FAM programme has been successful, resulting in extensive media coverage worldwide.

(Ministry of Tourism and Culture, 2014)

The initiatives and programmes undertaken by Tourism Malaysia have yielded a greater potential to serve as a cultural pivot and lynchpin of connectivity among nations. Malaysia aims to further increase tourist arrivals from India and has commenced sales mission operations in various cities in India. In March 2014, the Malaysia delegation, led by the Minister of Tourism Mohamed Nazri bin Abdul Aziz, traveled to India to host new marketing initiatives and attract tourists from India.[1] The sales mission is considered a platform for Malaysia's tourism industry players to strengthen their ties with the Indian counterparts as well as to strengthen Malaysia's stature as a dream destination among the people of India. The potential of India as an important market is reflected in the Memorandum of Understanding in Tourism signed in 2010 and the establishment of Tourism offices in Chennai, Mumbai and New Delhi.[2] In addition, Malaysia's favorable exchange rate has also made India a competitive holiday destination for Malaysians, while Malaysia's growing popularity as a venue for international events has generated interest among Indian event managers to make the country a destination for conventions, exhibitions, sports, concerts and cultural events.[3]

Moreover, to attract more Indian arrivals, Tourism Malaysia had also launched its Meetings, Incentives, Conventions and Exhibitions (MICE) campaign in India. Incentives including preferential airfares, special rates for accommodations and transportation, dissemination of information, and special discounts at various convention centres are provided to attract Indian corporates and trade associations to host MICE events in Malaysia. The contribution of India to the Malaysian MICE arrivals has been growing steadily. From only 7,351 MICE arrivals in 2001, the Indian arrivals went up to 18,543 in 2003.[4]

The Ministry of Tourism Malaysia also sees a huge market for attracting the Indian tourists in some niche areas such as packages for weddings and honeymoons, golf, and adventure. Among these, the wedding and honeymoon package is receiving much interest and has piqued the attraction among the Indians. Malaysia is growing in popularity as a dream destination for weddings or honeymoons. Some of the reasons could be attributed to Malaysia's proximity with India, green scenery, world-class infrastructure, and its multicultural society. Among the most preferred locations in Malaysia for weddings as well as honeymoons are Kuala Lumpur, Langkawi Island, Penang and Sabah. The Ministry of Tourism believes Malaysia provides the perfect setting for a wedding rich in the flavour and culture of Asia. Often being touted as a value for money destination, Malaysia also ranks favourably to the budget of the average wedding family in India.[5] The Indians have a pool of choices in terms of themes in conducting the wedding, such as city weddings, resort weddings, beach weddings and hillside weddings. For instance, according to a Tourism Malaysia officer, the office recently organized a wedding for a family consisting of 900 guests coming all the way from India for the wedding in Sabah. Recognizing the importance of the destination of wedding and honeymoon segment of India, a number of high-end hotels in Kuala Lumpur, Penang and Langkawi have employed Indian wedding coordinators to facilitate destination weddings. Furthermore, Tourism Malaysia also promotes and facilitates tailor-made deals and conducts specific road shows in India to further tap this market. This justifies why, in 2013, Malaysia won awards for Travel + Leisure organized by India, whereby Langkawi Island was picked as runner-up in the Best Honeymoon Destination segment among the Indian tourists, and the Best Green Destination.[6] As a whole, the Tourism Malaysia offices in India have emerged as dynamic organizations. The efforts made by the government to establish a home-based office have not only promoted tourism but also nurtured a better relationship with local industry.

Although the social and cultural aspects between Malaysia and India seem to be moving in the right direction, there are pockets of concern that still pose challenges. Among them is the need to increase the tourist flows from other cities besides Chennai in India and Kuala Lumpur. Kuala Lumpur and Chennai are known as sister cities given that a majority of ethnic Indians in Malaysia are Tamils, and so are the majority of South Indians in India. However, there are not many exchanges and cooperation taking place outside these two cities. Besides tourism activities, especially visiting temples in South India, this concept of sister cities could be extended to include north Indian cities such as those in the Punjab state. This would endear well with Malaysia since there is a significant number of Sikhs in Malaysia. Tourism Malaysia should also promote Malaysia beyond Kuala Lumpur and Genting Highlands. Given that Indians like soft adventures, theme parks, shopping malls, food and city centres, Malaysia Tourism could promote these programmes to further increase the volume. Besides this, the readiness of hoteliers in Malaysia accommodating Indian weddings is also taxing, especially when some of the hotels are not well equipped to cater to the Indian weddings.

Another avenue to improve the people-to-people connectivity is to accept Malaysia's culture, especially the Malay and Chinese component of the culture. It is important for India to understand that the Malay and Chinese culture comprises 93 percent of Malaysia's population. Hence, there could be collaboration between Malaysia's cultural centre such as *Istana Budaya* and ICC to capture the holistic culture of Malaysia. According to Moses (2012), the media sector also needs to work together, for example, by providing an editorial space on Malaysia–India so that people would understand the mutual cultures that both states share and have in common. By doing so, the information gap between Malaysia and India could be reduced. India media could also station correspondents in Malaysia, like Malaysia is doing. Malaysia has its official news reporter in New Delhi to provide information on India's development. According to the former prime minister of Malaysia, a lack of promotion between both countries is the cause of the knowledge gap.[7]

Besides this, issues like difficulty in getting approvals for some Malaysian flights to operate in India have posed a challenge. This has been the case for Air Asia Bhd, which is the region's biggest low-cost airline, and it was aiming to commence flight operations in India since 2013 as Air Asia India but has yet to obtain approvals from the Indian government. Air Asia India is a joint venture between Malaysia-based Air Asia (49 percent), Mumbai-based Tata Sons (30 percent) and New Delhi–based Arun Bahtia's Telstra (21 percent) (The Hindu 2014, 15). Air Asia Bhd faced various challenges, such as policy disputes, delay of approvals and objections from the Federation of Indian Airlines, which had delayed its plans to start operations (StarBiz, 7 March 2014). Besides this, other challenges that Air Asia faced in doing business with India was the unpredictability and lack of transparency in India's regulatory framework (NST, Business Times 2014). For example, Air Asia first applied to the Foreign Investment Promotion Board (FIPB) in February 2013 and received a formal approval in April 2013, followed by a No Objection Certificate (NOC) in September 2013. However, Air Asia India could not start its operations due to steep resistance from Indian carriers, especially IndiGo, and legal hurdles (The Hindu 2014, 15). It is clear that in case of Air Asia Bhd, which is trying to operate in India, that protection of national carriers takes precedence over a more rational assessment of the net national economic and social benefits from tourism and trade. Nevertheless, after a long-drawn struggle, it is reported that Air Asia India finally got approval and will start commercial operations on June 12, 2014.

Another area of improvement is the Visa on Arrival (VoA) that the Malaysia government introduced. This VoA facility was introduced in 2006 in conjunction with VMY 2007. This VoA was offered to visitors from eight countries, including India. Tourists were accorded the flexibility to apply for a visa upon arrival at the Malaysian airport. One of the reasons Malaysia introduced this VoA was also to attract the business community. However, based on Malaysian immigration reports, VoA attracted the wrong group of people. Out of 80,000 VoAs approved for India, only 30,000 tourists returned.[8] Many Indian tourists abused this VoA by overstaying in Malaysia and getting involved in drug cases and crimes. Hence, this VoA facility was revoked in 2010 (*The Star* 2018, 1). However, conjunction with the VMY 2014, Malaysia relaxed visa restrictions for tourists from India who were traveling to Malaysia through a third country, namely, Singapore and Thailand, and given one-week validity. There is also the issue of an increase in visa application fees by the Malaysian High Commission that could affect the tourist arrivals to Malaysia. Malaysia has increased the visa processing fee from INR1,000 to INR3,000 ever since it has outsourced the visa application to a private company. Although the appointment of this company is to create one single system and control visa applications, nevertheless the increase in the fee did not go well among the tourist agents in India. Whether the increase in visa processing fee would deter the tourist arrivals to Malaysia is yet to be seen, but the visa issue is always seen as one of the major issues in Malaysia–India relations.

CONCLUSION

Malaysia–India relations have always been premised on strong historical, social, and cultural linkages. This connection has not been undermined by the forces of globalization. On the other hand, both governments have used the cultural dimension to promote greater connectivity and people-to-people contacts through travel and tourism. With the shared history and cultural connections, Malaysia has expressed its determination to strengthen its relationship with India through broader cooperation and engagement, especially in economic and socio-cultural aspects. A rich network of personal relationships through travel, study, work, business, sports, and cultural exchanges has opened the doors of opportunity to forge better understanding and enhance deeper cultural appreciation between the two countries. The reduction in the costs of air travel and the increase in the frequency of flights have furthermore boosted the physical connectivity. Even though there have been some issues, such as India's citizenship law, that spurred relations between Malaysia and India, diplomatically, bilateral relations between the two countries remain good. It has not posed any threat to the bilateral relations that were established in 1957. The 2.7 million Indian diaspora in Malaysia provides a substratum of the mutually beneficial engagement between Malaysia and India in economic and social cultural aspects.

REFERENCES

Anon. (2012). Wooing Indians for 'healing holidays, *The Star, 25 December*: 16.

Anon. (12–14 April 2013). *Malaysia Country Report*. Paper presented at the UNWTO 25th CAP-CSA and UNWTO Conference on Sustainable Tourism Development, Hyderabad, India.

Anon. (17 September, 2013). "Najib: Health Tourism in Malaysia generated RM600million in revenue last year," *The Star*. Retrieved from http://www.thestar.com.my/Business/Business-News/2013/09/17/Najib-Health-tourism-in-Malaysia-generated-RM600m-in-revenue-last-year.aspx/

Anon. (2014). 1937 law stands in AirAsia's way, *New Straits Times*, 29 January: B2.

Anon. (2014). Airasia India aims to start operations in May, *The Star,* 7 March: 9.

Anon. (2014). Malaysia bags top honours at Travael+Leisure's travel awards, *The Star, 14 April*. Retrieved from www.thestar.com.my/Travel/Malaysia/2014/04/14/Triple-win-for-Malaysias-travel-sector/

Anon. (2014). Indian Cultural Centre, Kuala Lumpur, Director, Interview, 22 January.

Anon. (2014). Malaysia-India: People to People relations and education issues, Consul General, Consulate General of Malaysia for South India, Chennai. Interview, 27 May.

Anon. (2014). Role and Challenges of Malaysia Tourism in India, Senior Deputy Director, International Promotion Division (South Asia/West Asia/Africa), Malaysia Tourism Promotion Board. Interview, 27 March.

Dawn, S. K., & Pal, S. (2011). *Medical Tourism in India: Issues, Opportunities and Designing Strategies for Growth and Development.*

Horowitz, M. D., Rosensweig, J. A., & Jones, C. A. (2007). Medical Tourism: Globalization of the Healthcare Marketplace. *Medscape General Medicine (MedGenMed), 9*(4), 33.

Informant. (2014). Malaysia Tourism Board, Chennai, India. Interview, 28 May 2014.

Informant (Consulate General of Malaysia for South India). (2014). Malaysia High Commission, Chennai. Interview, 27 May 2014.

Informant (Director). (2014). Indian Cultural Centre, Kuala Lumpur, Interview, 22 January 2014.

Informant (Director). (2014). Malaysia Technical Cooperation Programme (MTCP). MTCP Secretariat, Policy & Strategy Planning, Wisma Putra, Ministry of Foreign Affairs, Putrajaya. Interview, 26 March 2014.

Informant (Director). (2014). Malaysia-India Tourism Cooperation, Malaysia Tourism Board, New Delhi, India. Interview, 22 May 2014.

Informant (Senior Deputy Director). (2014). International Promotion Division (South Asia/West Asia/Africa), Malaysia Tourism Promotion Board. Kuala Lumpur. Interview, 27 March 2014.

Informant (Senior Manager). (2014). Malaysia Healthcare Travel Council, Kuala Lumpur. Interview, 25 April 2014.

International Journal of Multidisciplinary Research, 1(3), 185–202.

Laporan Tahunan. (2012). *Tourism Malaysia.*

Malaysia Healthcare Travel Council. Retrieved 14 January 2020, from http://www .mhtc.org.my/en/healthcare-industry-in-malaysia.aspx.

Moses, B. (2012). *India-Malaysia People to People Contacts.* Paper presented at the Third ICWA-ISIS India Malaysia Strategic Dialogue, Sapru House, New Delhi, India.

Review of National Tourism Policy (Main Report). (2020). Ministry of Tourism Malaysia: 5.

Tourism Malaysia. Retrieved 9 January 2020, from http://corporate.tourism.gov.my/ research.asp?page=facts_figures

Tourism Malaysia. Wed in Malaysia for a Truly Asia Wedding (pp. 3–4). Kuala Lumpur.

NOTES

1. Interview with the Senior Deputy Director for International Promotion Division (South Asia/West Asia/Africa), Malaysia Tourism Promotion Board, Putrajaya on 27 March 2014 at 11:00 a.m.

2. See "India-Malaysia Bilateral relations," at http://www.aseanindia.com/wp -content/uploads/2012/12/India_Malaysia_Relations.pdf. Accessed on 17 February 2014.

3. Interview with Senior Deputy Director for International Promotion Division (South Asia/West Asia/Africa), Malaysia Tourism Promotion Board, Putrajaya on 27 March 2014 at 11:00 a.m.

4. See http://articles.economictimes.indiatimes.com/2004-0624/news/27367705 _1_tourism-malaysia-mice-destination-arrivals.

5. See Tourism Malaysia pamphlet, "Wed in Malaysia for a Truly Asia Wedding," pp 3–4.

6. http://www.thestar.com.my/Travel/Malaysia/2014/04/14/Triple-win-for-Malaysias-travel-sector/.

7. Interview with former prime minister of Malaysia on 9 May 2014 at 11:00 a.m.

8. Information gathered from Malaysia High Commission Office, New Delhi, India, on 23 May 2014.

Chapter 4

India–Malaysia Maritime Cooperation

A Missed Opportunity

Tharishini Krishnan

INDIA–MALAYSIA MARITIME RELATIONS: AN OVERVIEW

The Eastern Indian Ocean Region (EIOR) has experienced human interaction for many millennia, developing an interactive high-seas trade between many different regions today; the Southeast Asia (SEA) in South Asia (SA) is one paradigm. Historian Coedes calls the SEA the "Indianised states," whereas scholars such as Majumdar and Sarkar name the SEA Greater India or Further India (Prakash and Lombard, 1999: 163–164).

The India–Malaysia maritime nexus has its own particular sense of unity. Interaction co-existed from the beginning of the first millennium C.E., continuing steadily to the present and surviving European intervention from the 15th to the 19th century. As early as the 11th century, Malaysia has been on the receiving end of Indian sea voyages, such as Raja Chola and Kingdom of Pagan, for trading purposes. It was certain that, before the arrival of European powers, merchants of Gujarat, Malabar, Coromandel, and Bengal sailed independently east to the Malay Peninsula, establishing themselves as pioneer traders in the EIOR. Maritime relations between Malaya and India were not damaged, even with the entry of the Portuguese, Dutch, and British. The Malayan community had already established a positive relationship with the Indian merchants and no change of policy took place. Instead, maritime interactions continued to benefit participants in trading activities in the EIOR;

both countries appreciated one another to a deeper extent than the already co-existing maritime bond concealed within their deep-rooted cultural ties.

During the Cold War, the long-standing relationship between India and Malaysia underwent a brief interval, and most newly independent countries avoided entanglement between the US and the USSR. The intermission was also driven by the fact that the role of the Indian Navy was confined to coastal defence and heavily relied on the British Royal Navy. Economic development was a major focus, meaning that maritime structure was a self-sufficient maritime strategy. In addition, the Indo-China conflict 1962 and the Indo-Pakistan War in 1965 led India to pay less attention to Malaysia. Similarly, in Malaysia, military assistance was reliant on former colonial masters, and development initiatives were priority in the form of the economy and societal well-being of the nation. On the other hand, communist insurgency was impacting internal security. As a result, land forces formed the major military focus of the Malaysian government in order to deter the communist movement. Consequently, lesser emphasis was given to maritime cooperation between India and Malaysia.

However, both countries bonded through the Non-Aligned Movement (NAM), in which they discussed the safety and security of the EIOR. While promoting the NAM, India and Malaysia were also seen as active partners in boosting the Indian Ocean Region (IOR) as a zone of peace, free from nuclear proliferation, weapons of mass destruction (WMD), arms race, military build-up, or any other form of coercive activities that could contribute to the region's instability. After the end of the Cold War, the relationship was restored through India's Look East Policy (LEP), Phases 1 and 2. Phase 1 was established in the early 1990s focusing on economy, whereas Phase 2 was established in early 2000 and focused on enhancing defence (such as maritime security). The LEP was further revitalised and boosted through the Act East Policy (AEP) in 2014. Both the LEP and AEP represent an opportunity for India and Malaysia to capitalise on the desire to work on common maritime interests. Thus far, India and Malaysia have continued to postulate a cordial partnership in the maritime domain.

MIND THE GAP

Maritime security comprises extensive issues that pertain to the management of resources, both living and non-living, that have a critical bearing on many countries and require constant examination, which is particularly true for the EIOR. Rich in marine resources and other aquatic varieties, the ocean also contains hydrocarbon resources, crude oil, petroleum products and minerals. The ocean is also a major artery for international trade, with

40 percent passing through the Straits of Hormuz, 35 percent through the Straits of Malacca, and 8 percent through the Bab el-Mandab Straits. On the other hand, the sea supports 80 percent of the oil trade transit throughout the IOR. The strategic location of the ocean connecting the east and west of the world's major sea lines of communications (SLOCs) has led most states to build a strong toehold in the EIOR. The EIOR is also broadly categorised as a space for competition by China challenging India's position. This area also faces nontraditional maritime issues, including piracy, terrorism at sea, illicit activities, natural disasters, and environmental issues.

The complex intertwining issues show the gravity of concern surrounding seeking stability and security in the region. Many countries have realised that there is much to be gained through inter-state cooperation and little through unilateralism, which is even more apparent in the case of maritime security because of its universality. India and Malaysia understand this perspective and both states acknowledge the need to improve the volume of maritime cooperation; an effective policy prescription to achieve mutual beneficial goals is the decisive task. However, despite this strong awareness of the need to build robust maritime cooperation, the level of collaboration between these two entities has remained surprisingly low. In 1993, Malaysia became the first country in SEA to sign defence cooperation with India, subsequently establishing the Malaysia-India Defence Cooperation Meeting (MIDCOM). In 2007, India and Malaysia commemorated 50 years of diplomatic relations. In October 2010, the India–Malaysia engagement formed a yet stronger foundation through the establishment of their Strategic Partnership, which meant strengthening bilateral ties and enhancing further in areas such as the economy, security-defence, and socio-cultural dimensions. This includes exchange between defence ministers and military officials, together with cooperation in defence projects, and cooperation in combating terrorism by exchanging information. In 2015, during the ASEAN-India Summit and East Asia Summit visit, India issued an Enhanced Strategic Partnership. The latest in 2018, during MIDCOM held in Kuala Lumpur, a Memorandum of Understanding on United Nations Linkages were signed. However, comparably, the level of maturity in the relationship with actual attempts in shaping tangible cooperation have not been aligned. In other words, the bilateral cooperation between India and Malaysia should be coherent with current maritime threats that both countries face today in the EIOR. However, it appears that the bilateral engagement is overlooked in both countries and it is unclear the reason for this negligence.

Maritime security has become an area of significance for India and Malaysia; these oceanic neighbours and traditional partners need to identify factors that may discourage the existence, extent, and depth of a bilateral maritime cooperation. On this ground, this chapter first analyses the problems in achieving formal commitment between India and Malaysia. The chapter then examines the prospects of informal commitment and discusses the catalyst on maritime strategic thinking to gain a more accurate perspective on the reasons as to why building stronger bilateral relationships between India and Malaysia is temporised but requires urgent attention. Barry Buzan's Regional Security Complex Theory (RSCT) is used as a base to address the need for a strong bilateral cooperation between the two countries. Buzan argues that a "security complex" is when "a group of states whose primary security concerns link together sufficiently closely that their national securities cannot realistically be considered apart from one another" (Buzan, 1991). Security complexes can be useful in terms of policy and provide a good framework to discuss issues endemic to any one region. RSCT is significant in drawing a logical explanation of India–Malaysia maritime security in the EIOR. The lack of robustness in the engagement between India and Malaysia concurrently postulates that the two countries hold a limited understanding of their role and function as security partners in the region, despite both appreciating historical relations as well as their substantial ability to address the maritime security challenges in the EIOR, projecting a missed opportunity. Both countries have failed to securitise the security complexes that link them together. Hence, this chapter highlights the blindness in strategic maritime thinking across the relationship to strengthen the direction towards securitising bilateral cooperation between the two countries.

PROBLEMS FOR FORMAL BILATERAL COMMITMENT

Multilateral cooperation is an arrangement that takes into account the interests of a number of countries. Although multilateralism can be an advance for a stronger relationship, this kind of arrangement can often become biased wherein the stronger power can seek to dominate the weaker power in a grouping.

In mitigating nontraditional threats, for instance, there are several maritime security initiatives in the Malacca Straits. One of the most publicised initiatives is the Malacca Straits Coordinated Patrol (MALSINDO), which was established in July 2004. This patrol is a joint patrolling system amongst littoral states. Hence, there has been concern amongst littoral states on losing sovereignty in the process. Opting in to combined patrolling system is also a concern. Combined patrolling systems are usually used under the umbrella of a command structure with a singular code and conduct instructed by a sole power. Combined patrolling may face a number of issues, such as the balance of interoperability. Engaging with a stronger country may lead a weaker country to face domination in terms of command, which can cause distrust in the partnership. A stronger country may also feel that it is engaging in the partnership with little or no benefits in return as the weaker party will have less to offer. Malaysia, along with other littoral states, has declined India's assistance to be mindful of sovereignty issues. As a result, the combined patrolling system often met with disappointment, and thus explains the reasons for cooperation between both countries to remain stagnant. Similar situation is observed in the "Eyes in the Sky" programme, which is part of the broader Malacca Straits Security Initiative (MSSI), comprising Indonesia, Malaysia, and Singapore. As a combined patrolling effort initiated in 2005, the "Eyes in the Sky" is a programme to guard the Straits of Malacca from piracy. The initiative is expected to be an effective collaboration to curtail piracy attacks because it involves three major countries with authority in the area. However, as mentioned before, three countries would ensure that no single power dominated the arrangement.

Establishing joint patrolling between two interested parties is thus more efficient it creates an equal balance of benefits to both partners, and in the EIOR, with an increasing concern of piracy attacks and adjacent to the Bay of Bengal, there is a need for India's strong involvement. Bilateral cooperation can be viewed as a more effective choice of communication than multilateral commitment because it involves two individual countries with particular interests in hand. This type of cooperation can meet the needs of both countries equally in all areas, such as their roles, responsibilities, and interests, as well as the intended outcomes. In this way, cooperation may minimise disorientation in bilateral relationships and reduce distrust relating to issues and areas that constantly prevent more resilient cooperation, one dimension in which both India and Malaysia are lacking. In addition to the constraints engendered by the laws of the sea, members of MSSI face other political issues in the region which had an impact on engagement. Malaysia does not have overlapping territories or disputed maritime areas with India (whereas Malaysia does have disputes with Singapore over Pedra Branca; the Philippines, Vietnam, and China over the Spratly Islands; and Indonesia over Ambalat). India is an emerging power that has had a benign role thus far. Together with India's traditional partnership with Malaysia, bilateral cooperation between India and Malaysia could be easily shaped based on mutual maritime interest.

Bilateral cooperation on traditional issues is causing more anxiety, particularly for Malaysia. The underlying issue that discourages the possibility of a bilateral commitment is lack of trust, in that Malaysia still prefers to adopt multilateral engagement and avoid depending solely on one power or showing obvious balancing or bandwagoning behaviour. As a small country, a multilateral platform may be more viable. For example, India's engagement with Malaysia through the Association of Southeast Asian Nations (ASEAN) is effective (The United Service of India, group interview, 2015). With Malaysia as a small nation, ASEAN is a major instrument used to make collective decisions vis-à-vis issues pertaining to the region. However, it is important to note that collective decision-making is the principal characteristic of ASEAN and promotes a regional architecture of peace and security, being strongly reliant on mutual confidence building, dialogues, and transparency (The United Service of India, group interview, 2015). Participation in regional maritime institutions such as ASEAN Defence Minsters Meetings (ADMM) and the Indian Ocean Naval Symposium (IONS) builds habits of cooperation, mutual understanding, and confidence, while also creating spill over into bilateral relationships (The United Service of India, group interview, 2015). In other words, India and Malaysia's participation in multilateral regional maritime institutions has set a strong foundation for bilateral cooperation in the EIOR.

Hence, the option to cooperate bilaterally should be made possible. During the Cold War, India's habit of engaging bilaterally with the ASEAN was driven strongly by India's suspicious attitude towards the ASEAN platform. Although this mind-set is no longer common, there should be more constructive thinking with a focus on bilateral participation (The United Service of India, group interview, 2015). It is time to move into a bilateral framework to allow both countries to share their maritime expertise directly with one another, a move that would be strategically valuable for both countries (High Commission of India, personal communication, 2014). In terms of security or defence cooperation between India and Malaysia, more persuasion may be required. Malaysia's passivity towards engaging with India plays a part in the lack of bilateral engagement. Malaysia should be more assertive in engaging India in terms of defence cooperation as it is currently complacent about its mature, friendly relationship with India. As India, Singapore, and Indonesia all seek to have a blue water navy, Malaysia could further engage India and learn from India's experiences to achieve its ambition of becoming a blue water navy. Today, the prospect for such possibilities is more prominent with the presence of Quadrilateral Security Dialogue (Quad) under the Indo-Pacific confluence, in which India is a major driver.

In a meeting in November 2015, the Malaysian and Indian Prime Ministers stated that the Malaysian embassy in Delhi was one of the earliest to be established. However, the areas of agreement in the Malaysia–India bilateral relationship are confined largely to trade rather than defence (Maritime Department, Ministry of Foreign Affairs, personal communication, 2014). The agreement focuses on trade relations alone, and there is no bilateral mechanism for defence or security cooperation except through tASEAN, the ASEAN Regional Forum (ARF), and ADMM Plus. An India–Malaysia bilateral cooperation may subsequently help bolster both India's and Malaysia's positions in those multilateral institutions, giving more strength to the EIOR.

These multilateral engagements, particularly through ASEAN, although welcome, should not be the only means of achieving cooperation. Whilst common security challenges can be discussed as agendas in these regional multilateral platforms, the implementation of the agendas will fall back on the bilateral relationship if countries want a solid policy outcome. To boost an India–Malaysia bilateral engagement, a discussion of non-conventional threats faced by the two countries with a focus on relevant security levels may be a good starting point (The United Service of India, group interview, 2015).

It is believed that India would also welcome a more proactive relationship with Malaysia if Malaysia were to be enthusiastic about developing a larger maritime role for itself in the region. A bilateral mechanism for maritime cooperation is needed and critical for both navies in terms of talks and exercises (Ministry of Defence, group interview, 2014). Malaysia, despite projecting itself as a maritime nation in its recent Defence White Paper 2019, expresses a lack of enthusiasm towards a more resilient maritime power, unlike that of its neighbouring countries, such as Indonesia and Singapore, which appears to be the cause of disengagement on bilateral terms. Both bilateral and multilateral cooperation are critical components in shaping stability amongst the countries of the EIOR, and bilateral relations between India and Malaysia are no exception. However, an underlying element for greater success in shaping this cooperation lies in the ability of India and Malaysia to build a multilayered structure comprising navies, coast guards, and other related maritime agencies and forces. Each of these entities should set out their own roles and capabilities. A list of issues should be written down in terms of weapons, training, budgets, priorities, types of communication, and levels of commitment. This classification would help shape more effective and realistic cooperation.

Emphasis is required from both India and Malaysia. Both countries should test cooperation, namely regional, sub-regional, inter- and intra-regional, and with international organisations. India is considered to be a benign leader in the IOR and its major role in IONS and the Indian Ocean Rim Association (IORA) initiative is welcomed by many countries because of its prospects in enhancing maritime security cooperation in the IOR. Significant potential exists from both sides to improve international cooperation to strengthen security in the region and create a broad-based IOR security strategy that is acceptable to all. India has already engaged in a number of regional maritime programs with Malaysia, and their diplomatic ties are mature (High Commission of India in Kuala Lumpur, personal communication, 2014). As such, the prospect for bilateral arrangement is high for India and Malaysia because the two countries have established a strong relationship for centuries and adopted cooperative outlooks in their overall foreign policies.

BUILDING THE BRIDGE

One of the methods that could be used to achieve this objective is to shape informal bilateral and multilateral networks to increase trust and understanding between the two countries. These networks can also reduce the costs of building, and if a certain level of understanding is not achieved, a decision to dissolve further cooperative relationships may be made. The network begins with an informal platform with ad hoc groupings that may gradually be formalised towards more mature, structured groupings similar to other established bilateral and multilateral arrangements. This informal network is flexible, but it does not mean that it has no essence in framework or objective. Simply increasing the number of informal bilateral agreements within the region expands the network and binds regional states more tightly into ever-greater cooperation. In short, this kind of cooperation is part of the progress towards a more profound, refined cooperation amongst countries.

The annual Cobra Gold military exercise held in Thailand is one model established in 1982 as a bilateral maritime warfare exercise between Thailand and the US. In 1999, Singapore joined this agreement because of its positive relationship with the US and has been receiving more participation ever since, attracting countries such as Mongolia, Philippines, China, and Japan. Today, Cobra Gold is recognised as one of those groupings that has followed an informal structure and later grown into the region's most established formal multilateral cooperation network. In 2014, over 13,000 service members from the US, Thailand, Japan, Indonesia, Malaysia, Singapore, and South Korea participated, with China participating in humanitarian projects and other nations, including Myanmar's, observers (Parameswaran, 2015). Though it became a multilateral engagement, a similar approach is possible between India and Malaysia to shape formal bilateral engagements. A leadership role is required in India to show greater confidence in its maritime relationship with Malaysia in the EIOR.

The network involving Japan, Malaysia, and the Philippines is another example. Japan's maritime interests in the region may be seen through the Japanese coast guard partnership with members of SEA states. While Malaysia is a vital power in the Straits of Malacca, the Philippines is a key player in the South China Sea (SCS). Japan has attempted to engage with these two countries on two different issues, namely antipiracy training with the Philippines Coast Guard and the reorganisation of the maritime security force structure of Malaysia (and Indonesia) to establish a coast guard (Parameswaran, 2015). Bilateral relationships with Japan are growing stronger; as they mature, they will naturally develop into a network through which the Malaysian and Philippine coast guards will develop greater trust in and understanding of each other through common involvement with the Japanese (Parameswaran, 2015). India has a range of capabilities and profound knowledge of maritime activities. Japan's initiatives can be taken as a model to replicate similar cooperation with Malaysia in the EIOR.

However, a number of concerns remain. Countries that form arrangements in the shape of informal cooperation also seek long-term benefits. Although informal arrangements can be dissolved at little cost, the efforts taken to establish cooperation is wasted without an effective plan for execution. An adequate investigation into the history of relative relationships, capabilities, and roles is essential in creating a strong foundation for an informal arrangement before it is converted into a formal bilateral or multilateral cooperation. In mitigating nontraditional issues, cooperation is more easily shaped and the costs are low in contrast to dealing with traditional issues, which demands a higher cost. Table talks are common amongst countries. Therefore, these kinds of platform countries have the liberty to express their needs on certain issues, particularly when matters involve two specific countries is one way. As a sovereign state, distrust may be present in dialogues, but it is important to acknowledge that a lack of trust is not an obstacle to cooperation. Maritime security is universal in character; in the era of globalisation, maritime security is one particular area that requires a stronger push for further cooperation amongst countries.

When countries identify the interests and factors that deter their objectives, both formal and informal arrangements can illustrate their potential. There is a need to reanalyse Malaysia's defence and security policy with India (Institute for Defence Studies and Analyses, group interview, 2015). Exploring different types of maritime clustering would be a good start. The sub-regional link in the Bay of Bengal is one example linking the Andaman Sea with east-central India. The bay also abuts Myanmar and is a common ground for both India and Malaysia in the EIOR. The entire area of the Malacca Strait and the Andaman Sea comprises the territorial sea and the Exclusive Economic Zone (EEZ) and continental shelf of the littoral states (Singh, n.d.). This area should act as an incentive for promoting regional maritime cooperation. The overlapping structure means that no single state can truly dominate. Therefore, cooperation should be easy; as noted, India and Malaysia have no disputes, instead only sharing a common playground.

Another formation has been by separating high-intensity issues involving arms, drugs, and human smuggling, which have a direct impact on national security, from low-intensity issues such as illegal fishing, pollution, and ecological damage. Other clusters may be around ad hoc cooperation in response to emergency events or conflicts such as natural disasters. These clusters may slowly grow towards intra-regional, inter-regional, and mid-level cooperation on a multilateral, trilateral, or bilateral level to finally form a strategic cooperation. A clear direction of maritime purpose would solve the implementation of India–Malaysia bilateral cooperation in the EIOR. The structure should focus on specific elements, such as a state's quality and capability, its geographical location during crisis and peacetime, its influence in specific issues, its historical relationships with allies and adversaries, its current geopolitical scenario, and its domestic conditions. A clear grasp of these elements would help both India and Malaysia in understanding one another's maritime interests and shaping a stronger bilateral cooperation in the EIOR.

UNLOCKING MARITIME STRATEGIC THINKING

India's and Malaysia's commitment towards bilateral cooperation, both formal and informal, requires a dramatic change in maritime strategic thinking. In other words, there is a vital need for a breakthrough in the maritime relationship between India and Malaysia. The opinion prevalent in the top echelons of the Malaysian government is that the relationship between the two countries is mature and thus only requires maintenance. Regular Navy to Navy Staff Talks were held. India–Malaysia maritime interactions were also seen through MILAN, INDOPURA and SAREX naval exercises. India also took part in the mechanism of cooperation in the Straits of Malacca and Singapore, and contributed to two of the six projects, the International Maritime Organization (IMO) (Project 1 and Project 4), to improve the safety of navigation and environmental protection at the Malacca Straits. India also signed the annual MIDCOM, and conducts regular visits to Malaysian ports for capacity building and patrolling pirate-infested areas at sea for drug trafficking, human trafficking, and maritime terrorism. India has made strong attempts at engagement with Malaysia: naval visits, dialogues, capacity building, and coordinated patrolling to face the increasing maritime challenges, especially transnational challenges such as drug trafficking, human trafficking, piracy and terrorism.

Malaysia has been actively sending officers and men for various courses, including SUKHOI and the SCORPENE expertise, gunnery, and submarine specialisation (Ministry of Defence, group interview, 2014), and more specifically to note, in 2014 India provided assistance to Malaysia and deployed six ships and five aircraft to undertake search operations in the Bay of Bengal after the incident of MH370. All these signal that relationship has postulated a satisfactory position. Nevertheless, several of these bilateral arrangements are not enshrined in official agreements. Strategic partnership is often used as a benchmark for analysing the intensity of state interactions in international relations. In this case, India–Malaysia relations can be categorised as *a missed opportunity* (Singh, 2011: 87).

Hence, it is clear to both nations that the relationship between India and Malaysia needs a more specific focus (The United Service of India, group interview, 2015; Ministry of Defence, group interview, 2014). Therefore, India and Malaysia should be proactive and not stick to meetings, consultations and forums per se. Concurrently, it is Malaysia that has not engaged with India in a more proactive manner. It has been stated that Malaysia's Secretary General has reminded bureaucrats to "not forget India" (Ministry of Defence, group interview, 2014); he has reemphasised that India is incredibly important to Malaysia and remarked that it is unfortunate that Malaysia's positive relationship with India is not common knowledge (Ministry of Defence, group interview, 2014). Therefore, it is time for a vital shift in strategic thinking in Malaysia to ensure a sounder, pronounced maritime relationship with India.

India has already particular interest in the SEA region through its LEP and AEP. India's unique position in the SEA and IOR, as well as the wider context of Indo-Pacific Region, is advantageous to Malaysia but dependent on Malaysia and what it can offer to attract India to engage further (High Commission of India, personal communication, 2014). Malaysia's reaction to and engagement with India says a lot about Malaysia's acknowledgment of India's efforts, meaning the way in which Malaysia is reacting and engaging is where most answers lie (Institute for Defence Studies and Analyses, group interview, 2015). Furthermore, Malaysia's active reaction will signal India to reciprocate. Therefore, Malaysia should show more commitment to recognise India as a crucial power in creating a new power structure in the EIOR. India may seem preoccupied with internal and regional politics and conflict with Pakistan, thus demurring from outreach engagement. This potential attitude should not, however, be seen as a deterrent to other countries, particularly Malaysia. Therefore, if Malaysia engages with India, India will be able to reciprocate and form stronger relations in maritime with Malaysia in the areas of energy cooperation, shipbuilding, and maintenance, as well as the safety of the Straits of Malacca, the Andaman and Nicobar Islands, and the Bay of Bengal. Hypothetically, if Malaysia's power projection in the EIOR is contingent on Kuala Lumpur's change of security focus, then a role for further, deepened Malaysia–India maritime security cooperation can be foreseen. For this situation to materialise, serious proactive engagement is required.

The maritime relationship between India and Malaysia is currently stalled and needs an overhaul to adapt to the changing environment in the IOR (Malaysia Maritime Enforcement Agency, personal communication, 2014). Political will is a vital driver in any relationship, and the India–Malaysia maritime cooperation is no exception. There is significant potential, particularly in the Straits of Malacca (The United Service of India, group interview, 2015) and Bay of Bengal, under the Indo-Pacific strategy. Therefore, it may be necessary to reanalyse Malaysia's relationship with India. Given that India and Malaysia have a long-standing, mature relationship, there is a need to evolve and redefine this relationship, particularly in the maritime domain in the EIOR. With this in mind, Malaysia should first position itself and gain leverage for the specific purpose of sustainability before engaging with India. For example, Malaysian navies lack equipment, which must first be addressed; focusing on navy logistics is vital to create a shift in the relationship, where India is viewed as a necessary partner (Ministry of Defence, group interview, 2014). The 15 to 5 programmes have stalled due to ineffective management, which has negatively impacted plans for new procurement purchase. Most of the Malaysian navy's assets are also aging. If these problems are addressed acutely, Malaysia, when engaging on technical and logistics assistance, could be pivotal in its assertion of its need for cooperation from India in maritime security in the EIOR. More of this kind of manoeuvre can be foreseen only with changes to the overall mind-set.

Therefore, the strong convergence of mutual interest is vital to any cooperation or relationship (The United Service of India, group interview, 2015). In the case of India and Malaysia, the need for cooperation does not seem to be solid or convincing enough for either party to initiate proceedings; maritime blindness is the major stumbling block. There is a need for Malaysia in particular with the scenario in the SCS, where Malaysia tends to be friendlier towards India than China as balancer or an alternative. India should also show an equal amount of commitment in order to gain Malaysia's trust. India should continue to maintain that any diplomatic cooperation is sought only for the safety and security of the SLOCs and not with the objective of dominating or projecting power in these areas (Maritime Department, Ministry of Foreign Affairs, personal communication, 2014). As such, India's maritime effort being focused eastward is of greater importance. Subsequently, the gaps between India and Malaysia will be reduced and their relationship will be strengthened.

CONCLUSION

The purpose of this chapter was to revitalise India–Malaysia maritime security cooperation. Whilst there are many methods that may be employed to address this standpoint, this chapter discussed issues and challenges of both formal and informal bilateral and multilateral commitments, an aspect that is often neglected but vital in forming stronger maritime cooperation between both countries. However, the major issue has been the "credible commitments" from both countries, which are essential in shaping a solid bilateral relationship between India and Malaysia. At the moment, India and Malaysia are generally viewed as long-standing allies in the maritime domain, but they have not shown any remarkable or stimulating cooperation in the region. For nations that have commemorated approximately more than 50 years of diplomatic relations, the maritime relationship between the two is subdued.

It is strongly suggested that a fundamental change in maritime strategic thinking is the key to revitalising the relationship. This change requires Malaysia to change its position and be more forward thinking (The United Service of India, group interview, 2015). This realisation will uplift efforts toward securitising the maritime concern between the two countries and shape convergence. Working hand in hand in line with the evolution of cultural thinking between the two countries is a major contributing factor towards the success or failure of the bilateral relationship. Culture has been a major characteristic in the study of social sciences. In the field of international study, this characteristic has been embedded strongly, particularly in understanding state interactions that comprise two different cultures. Similarly, in analysing national security policy, culture plays a prominent role because different cultural backgrounds impact a state's foreign policy behaviour or outcomes inversely, which here refers to strategic culture thinking in the maritime domain. Subsequently, this focus will provide more promising opportunities in the future of India–Malaysia maritime security cooperation.

REFERENCES

Abdullah, Ahmad. 1987. *Tengku Abdul Rahman and Dasar Luar Malaysia: 1963–1970*. Kuala Lumpur: Benton Publishing Sdn. Bhd.

Albert, Lau. 2012. *Southeast Asia and the Cold War*. London: Routledge.

Amitendu Palit, A. 2016. India's Act East Policy and Implications for Southeast Asia. *Southeast Asian Affairs* (2016): 81–92.

Arasaratnam, Sinnappah. 1994. *Maritime India in the Seventeenth Century*. Delhi: Oxford University.

Arasaratnam, Sinnappah. n.d. *Dutch Commercial Policy and Interest in the Malay Peninsula, 1750–795. Malaysia: NUS Press.*

Ashin, Das Gupta. 1994. *Merchants of Maritime India, 1500–1800*. Great Britain: Variorum.

Babbage, Ross and Sam Bateman. 1993. *Maritime Change: Issues for Asia.* Singapore: Allen & Unwin, and Royal Australian Navy and Australian Defence Industries Ltd.

Bhaswati, Bhattacharya. 1999. *The Chulia Merchants of Southern Coromandel in the 18th Century: A Case for Continuity. In Om Prakash and Denys Lombard, eds. 1999. Commerce and Culture in the Bay of Bengal 1500–1800. New Delhi: Rajkamal Electric Press.*

Buzan, Barry. 1991. *People, State and Fear. An Agenda for International Security Studies in the Post-Cold Era. Wheatsheaf Books Ltd.*

Buzan, Barry and Ole Waever. 2003. *Region and Powers: The Structure of International Security. Cambridge: Cambridge Law Press.*

Chong Guan, Kwa and John Skogan. 2007. *Maritime Security in Southeast Asia.* London: Routledge.

Cohen, Stephen. 1991. *India Briefing-India as a Great Power: Perceptions and Prospects.* Boulder: Westview Press.

Emmers, Ralf. 2010. *Maritime Security in Southeast Asia.* In Sumit Ganguly, Andrew Scobell and Joseph Chinyong. 2010. *The Routledge Handbook of Asian Security Studies.* London: Routledge.

Ginifer, Jeremy. 1994. *Multinational Naval Force Structures.* In Michael Pugh. 1994. *Maritime Security and Peacekeeping: A Framework for United Nations Operations.* Manchester: Manchester University Press.

Goldrick, James and Jack MacCaffrie. 2013. *Navies of South-East Asia: A Comparative Study. London: Routledge.*

Holmes, James, Andrew Winner, and Toshi Yoshihara. 2009. *Indian Naval Strategy in the Twenty-first Century. London: Routledge.*

Kanti, Bajpai, and Amitabh Mattoo. 2000. *The Peacock and the Dragon: India-China Relations in the 21st Century. New Delhi: Har-Anand Publications Pvt. Ltd.*

Malone, David. 2011. *Does the Elephant Dance? Contemporary Foreign Policy.* Oxford: Oxford University Press.

Narayan Chaudari, Kirti. 1985. *Trade and Civilisation in the Indian Ocean: An Economic History from the Rise of Islam to 1750. London: Cambridge University Press.*

Nye, Joseph. 2008. *The Powers to Lead.* New York: Oxford University Press.

Pamulaparthi Venkata Rao. 2010. Indian Ocean Maritime Security Cooperation: The Employment of Navies and Other Maritime Forces. *Journal of the Indian Ocean Region* 6(1): 129–137.

Pant, Harsh. 2008. *Contemporary Debates in Indian Foreign and Security Policy.* New York: Palgrave Macmillan.

Pant, Harsh. 2011. *Indian Strategic Culture: The Debate and its Consequences.* Handbook of India's International Relations. London: Routledge.

Pant, Harsh. 2012. *The Rise of the Indian Navy: Internal Vulnerabilities, External Challenges. Burlington: Ashgate.*

Pant, Harsh. 2012. *Indian Ocean in Focus.* In Geoffrey Till and Patrick Bratton, eds. 2012. *Sea Power and the Asia Pacific: The Triumph of Neptune.* New York: Routledge.

Parameswaran, Prashanth. 2015. US-Thailand Relations and Cobra Gold 2015: What's Really Going On? *The Diplomat.* https://thediplomat.com/2015/02/u-s -thailand-relations-and-cobra-gold-2015-whats-really-going-on/.

Prakash, Om and Denis Lombard, eds. 1999. *Commerce and Culture in the Bay of Bengal, 1500–1800.* Manohar/Indian Council of Historical Research.

Sakhuja, V. 2006. *Indian Navy: Keeping Pace with Emerging Challenges.* In Prabkabar, L. W., Ho, J. H., and Bateman, S., eds. 2006. *The Evolving Maritime*

Balance of Power in the Asia Pacific: Maritime Doctrines and Nuclear Weapons at Sea. Singapore: Institute of Defence and Strategic Studies, Nanyang Technological University.

Sakhuja, Vijay. 2011. *Asian Maritime Power in the 21st Century: Strategy Transactions, China, India and Southeast Asia. Project Muse. Institute of Southeast Asian Studies Publishing Limited.*

Scott, David. 2007. Strategic Imperatives of India as an Emerging Player in Pacific Asia. *Journal of International Studies* 44(2): 123–140.

Scott, David. 2009. India's Extended Neighbourhood Concept: Power Projection for a Rising Power. *India Review* 8(2): 107–143.

Shankar Menon, Shiv. 2010. Maritime Imperatives of Foreign Policy, Maritime Affairs. *Journal of the National Maritime Foundations of India* 5(2): 15–21.

Sikri, Veena. 2013. *India and Malaysia: Intertwined Strands.* New Delhi: Ajay Kumar Jain for Manohar Publishers & Distributors.

Singh, Amit. 2011. India-Malaysia Strategic Relations. *Maritime Affairs: Journal of the National Maritime Foundation of India 7(1): 85–105.*

INTERVIEWS

(The interviews were carried out with the consent of the interviewees in anonymity.)

High Commission of India, 2014. Personal Communication.

Institute for Defence Studies and Analyses. 2015. Group Interview.

Malaysia Maritime Enforcement Agency, 2014. Personal Communication.

Maritime Department, Ministry of Foreign Affairs. 2014. Personal Communication.

Ministry of Defence Malaysia. 2014. Group Interview.

United Service of India. 2015. Individual and Group Interviews.

Chapter 5

One Identity, Two Realities

Social Issues Among the Sikhs in Malaysia and Punjab, India

Sarjit S. Gill, Charanjit Kaur, and K. Puvaneswaran

INTRODUCTION

Diaspora is a community of people living or settled permanently in other countries, aware of their origins and identity and maintaining various degrees of contact with the home country. The diaspora of many ethnic groups is found around the world today and ethnic Punjabi Sikhs are no exception. There are close to 5 million (East) Punjabis worldwide; over one-quarter of Indian migrants are from a region that constitutes a mere 2 percent of the national population (Taylor, et al., 2007). Others estimate that there are over 25 million Sikhs worldwide and roughly one-third live outside Punjab[1] (Dusenbery, 1997). Generally, migration activities are associated with domestic economic challenges, but they are also no exception to social remittances in the form of ideas, values, beliefs and practices. The Sikh community living outside of their real or perceived "homelands" is the main source of cultural diversity today across the globe and certainly in Malaysia. With the advancement of new technology and communications, it allows diasporas to play a role without returning to their home countries. Therefore, there are many Sikhs around the world who preserve their identity by retaining strong ties with their country and culture of origin but at the same time are flexible to adopt a new culture of the new country the migrated to or born in.

Whilst the Sikh communities living all over the world seek to preserve their unique and fundamental culture from potential mutation, assimilation, or conflict, they are also hampered by social issues that are rarely discussed in the public sphere. It is common knowledge that Sikhs all over the world have a uniform way of life based on the philosophy of *Guru Granth Sahib*. Through the code of conduct of *Sikh Rehat Maryada* (SRM), Sikhs are organized in an egalitarian system where gender, age, race or nationality differences are not important. However, most of the social issues plaguing the Sikh community are largely based on the social inequalities that revolve around family institutions. Therefore, this chapter discusses the social problems experienced by the Sikhs in two different countries, namely Malaysia and Punjab, India. Although the Punjabi Sikh ethnicity has clear similarities, especially in terms of religious identities, such as *Khalsa* and the *5K symbol,* nevertheless each experiences a different social situation. As a minority ethnic, Sikhs in Malaysia see the plight of family institutions that play less of a role in upholding the Punjabi language and experiencing the dilemma of intermarriage. Despite the majority status, the Sikh community in Punjabi, on the other hand, especially the youths, are easily trapped in drug abuse and experience the issue of unemployment. However, both societies face similar social issues, namely alcoholism and ambiguity of religious identity, which shows that the philosophy of the Sikh religion is not fully appreciated by the Sikhs in both countries.

SIKH PHILOSOPHY: AN OVERVIEW

Sikhism was initiated[2] over 550 years ago and its approach to life is realistic, therefore it is most contemporary, practical and rational in practice (Kaur, 2012). *Sikhism* perceived spiritual guidance from *Guru Granth Sahib* (scripture) and its philosophy well ahead of its time. *Guru Granth Sahib* is an authentic scripture, and the author is God Himself, who revealed the truth to the Sikh Gurus[3] (messenger of God) and ordained them to spread it to mankind all over the globe. Sikh spirituality is centred around the necessity of understanding and experiencing God and eventually becoming one with God. It is a guide to the Sikh ideal way of life that emphasizes selfless action carried out in society's best interests, and promotes normal family life and social commitment. Sikhs are also administered by their code of conduct, *Sikh Rehat Maryada*. The *Sikh Rehat Maryada* entails an ideal lifestyle for a Sikh as preached in the teachings of the Sikh holy scripture, *Guru Granth Sahib*, together with Sikh traditions and conventions. The *Sikh Rehat Maryada* identifies how to live a *Sikhi* lifestyle, with precise do's and don'ts to maintain a good, pure Sikh life as lined by the Gurus. For that reason, the Shiromani Gurdwara Parbandhak Committee (SGPC), Amritsar, defines the Sikh as: "Any human being who faithfully believes in One immortal being, ten Gurus, the *Guru Granth Sahib*, the utterances, and teachings of the ten

Gurus and the baptism bestowed by the tenth Guru, and who does not owe allegiance to any other religion" (Kaur, 2003).

Sikhs are encouraged to embed three main domains into their social life, namely social equality, reject any form of caste discrimination, and lead a *seva* (selfless/community service) centred life. According to Thakar (2016), a *Khalsa* (initiated or baptized Sikh) is the ideal definition of a Sikh in *Sikh Rehat Maryada*. In general, the community takes pride of their external identity as it "provides an impressive image of an agile and striking looking persona, particularly when he is attired in a well-tailored uniform" (Kapur & Misra, 2003: 107). The 5Ks make up the most visible form of identity for Sikhs around the globe to date and unite them as a community (Singh, 2000). The 5Ks are physical exclusivities for the Sikh community, which directly differentiates them from the non-Sikhs. Baptized Sikhs are called *Khalsa* and required to wear 5K—physical symbols.[4]

Khalsa is expected to serve the community, defend the oppressed and provide leadership to the wider Sikh community (Sikh Coalition, 2008: 2). The Sikhs are enlightened to live a virtuous and true life while maintaining a balance between their spiritual and temporal obligations. Sikhism also preaches spirituality and inculcates the love for God, truthful living, universal brotherhood, peaceful co-existence, loyalty, justice, impartiality, honesty, humility, forgiveness, self-control, courage, contentment, tolerance and all other moral and virtues known to any holiest man in this world (Kaur, 2017). These virtues can be practiced through four simple methods which are synonymous to Sikhs' way of life: (i) *kirat karo* (work hard honestly), (ii) *wand chakko* (share your earnings with the needy ones), (iii) *naam japo* (contemplate—remember God in mind, words and actions) and (iv) *seva* (voluntary selfless service of humanity). Meanwhile, Kapur and Misra (2003) identified the following images that portray the Sikh community: (i) spiritual—focuses on humility, harmony and community (selfless) service (*seva*); (ii) heroic or bravery—derives from the history of oppression the Sikh community has faced; (iii) aesthetic (cultural traditions). Moreover, Sikh individuals are not isolated but are instead connected to the family (*parivaar*), society (*samaj*) and community congregation (*sadh-sangat*) (Sandhu, 2004).

SIKH COMMUNITY IN MALAYSIA

In Malaysia, Sikhs are known as a minority community living in the scripture, believing and practicing the teachings of *Guru Granth Sahib* (Kaur, 2012: 341). Sikhs comprise about 80,000 of the total Malaysian population of 32 million. They have been a respected minority for their historical contributions in maintaining peace, law and order, especially under the British rule since

1873 (Gill, 2005). Along with their contributions to Malaysia's economy and social development as noteworthy to and recognized by the government, most importantly, their presence has shaped the plural and multicultural society in Malaysia.

The Malay States were one of the localities where Sikh soldiers made their presence felt, besides other places such as Fiji, New Zealand, Australia, and Canada (Cohen, 1997). In general, farmers in Punjabi who are facing economic problems are attracted to Captain Speedy's invitation to work in the Malay States. He had much knowledge of the prowess of the Sikhs, spoke fluent Hindi and served in the armed forces in India before he commenced duties in Penang (Gullick, 1953). Most Sikh male migrants originated from the densely populated districts of Jalandhar, Ludhiana, Hoshiarpur, Faridkot and Gurdaspur (Malhi, 2015). However, Captain Speedy brought in 110 Sikhs from Punjab to resolve the Chinese secret society clashes in the 1870s over tin mining issues in Larut (Patrick, 1963). Most of the early Sikh migrants entering Malaya were males as Captain Speedy did not permit the sepoys to bring their wives and children to the Malay States. As a result, only 19 percent of Sikh women arrived in 1921 while only a very few Sikh immigrants arrived in Malaya with families until after World War II (Sandhu, 1969).

The Sikhs formed the backbone of the police and paramilitary forces of colonial Malaya, including the Malay States Guides (MSG), which was a military regiment formed in 1896, at least until 1914 and were numerically second only to the Malays before World War II (Sandhu 1969: 288). British officials in the Straits Settlements, including Governor Andrew Clarke, were impressed by the qualities of these Sikhs from Punjab. They were tall and possessed extraordinary strength. They stood no less than 5 feet 8 inches in height, were sturdy and well built. This caused their physical prowess to be well known throughout the Malay States, compared to other races, such as the Malays, Chinese and Indians. Although there were some amongst the other races that had similar physical attributes, they were not willing to endure working long hours beneath the scorching sun and being reprimanded by the British police officers. The involvement of the Sikhs in the colonial British security forces has strongly coloured the history of the coming of the Sikh community to Malaya. The success of the British in evolutionarily controlling Malaya demonstrates the vital importance of the Sikhs and this is an undeniable fact. The Sikhs proved to be the motivating factor that helped the British spread their control over areas which could be profitable for their traders.

Today, Sikhs in Malaysia venture into various fields of employment such as business and as professionals and government officials. Interestingly, many Sikh women are also active in increasing the country's productivity. Over the past 20 years, more Sikh individuals have ventured into politics, especially as members of the opposition. In 2018, Gobind Singh Deo was appointed as the Minister of Communications and Multimedia, who is responsible for information, personal data protection, film and media industry, international broadcasting and so on. Nevertheless, a career as a police officer is still popular among Malaysian Sikhs where a senior ranking Sikh police officer, Amar Singh, was appointed as the Director of Federal Commercial Crime Investigation Department, who is entrusted to investigate the high-profile case of 1Malaysia Development Berhad (1MDB). Interestingly, many Sikh women also served as crime-busters in white-collar crime, domestic abuse, cyber crimes, and violent crimes, to name a few. In other aspects, the Sikhs in Malaysia maintain their religious identity with unequivocal participation in religious and social activities at the local gurdwaras. The gurdwara is seen as a socio-religious institution to ensure that the Sikh religious values are trans- mitted to a new generation. Although small in numbers, the Sikh community contributes significantly to Malaysia's nation-building efforts.

SIKH COMMUNITY IN PUNJAB, INDIA

Punjab is a region located in the northwest of the Indian subcontinent. Despite centuries of a large Punjabi diaspora and migration, as of 2020, the major- ity of the world's 30 million Sikhs live in the Punjab region of India, where Sikhism traces its roots. Almost every Sikh is a Punjabi, while not every Punjabi is a Sikh. Punjabi is an ethnic group that originated from Punjab as Indo-Aryans of North India, while Sikhs are a religious cluster which complies *Sikhi* way of life. Sikhs constitute 1.9 percent (about 20 million) of India's one-billion-plus population (Census 2001). Of the Sikh population of over 19 million, more than 80 percent live in Punjab, the rest being either settled in India's large metropolitan cities of Delhi, Mumbai and Kolkata or scattered across the country. In Punjab, the Sikhs constitute a majority community which consists of Jats (landlords), Ravidasi and Mzahabi Sikhs (landless class), Ramgarhias (artisans, carpenters and others) and urbanized Khatri Sikhs.

The Sikhs of Punjab have witnessed alternating periods of non-violent and violent forms of struggle in their quest for identity, survival and political power from the founding of their faith in the 15th century by Guru Nanak (1469–1539) until today. According to Brubaker (2006), the dispersion can be defined as any and every nameable population category that is to a certain extent displaced in space. That being the case, millions of people were dis- placed first by the 1947 partition of India and Pakistan. Subsequently, Punjab witnessed violence and later by the restructure of Punjab motherland in the year 1966 along linguistic and religious lines. During the Green Revolution in the mid-1960s, Punjab's agricultural industry was able to produce much larger quantities of food with the introduction of chemical fertilizers, synthetic herbicides and pesticides. Consequently, Punjab has been popularly known as the "breadbasket of India," indicating high levels of productivity and growth in agriculture. Such a title seemed fitting until the late 1980s when even though the per capita income remained among the highest in the country, the growth in agriculture in Punjab "levelled off" (Chaturvedi, 2010). The advancement of the Green Revolution gave pressure to the small farmers and landless workers who could not afford the better-quality seeds and manure, besides many tenant farmers were evicted by their landlords because of the use of mechanization. As a result, Punjab's growth and productivity have not improved social development (Purewal, 2010), and inconsistencies between economic and social development are behind more than one century of resettling (Singh, 2008)—a persistent condition.

Sikhs in Punjab are among the most migrating to foreign countries due to economic pressures. Most of the younger generation is less interested in venturing into agriculture and remain unemployed despite having good academic qualifications (Kaur, 2015). Malaysia is one of the dream destinations that promise better a income besides Canada, United Kingdom, Australia and the United States of America. However, many of those with low qualifications experience harsh working environments such as low wages, long working hours, dirty jobs and no working insurance. As a result, Punjab is losing its expensive human resources—skilled and trained professionals like doctors, engineers, accountants and so on. Since fathers and/or sons of the family are the ones who move to the city or other states/countries to get better jobs, the farmlands lack the care and hands that it requires for good results. Henceforth, Punjab is receiving many labourers from neighbouring states to work on the land who are socially backward, illiterate and unskilled. The current reality of Punjab's social wellbeing is badly affected by the lower living and unhygienic conditions of the seasonal migrant labourer. Not only do they disturb the Punjabi Sikhs' social values and norms, but they are also the main carrier of cheap drugs and different types of diseases and infections and uneven forms of crime (Kaur, 2015).

SOCIAL ISSUES AMONG THE SIKHS IN MALAYSIA AND INDIA: A BRIEF LITERATURE REVIEW

Studies on social problems in Malaysia are largely focused on the majority group, especially the Malay society (Siwar and Kasim, 1997), that they directly neglect the importance of studying the minority groups such as the Sikhs. This can be partly validated when it is found that research on social issues in Malaysia has been focused on Malays in rural areas and migrants in urban areas in Malaysia (Nair, 2009). This is a string of perceptions of the general public and national leaders who are too optimistic about the lives of the Sikhs to the point of denying that they can also face family, economic and social problems. Although there are many studies[5] conducted by local researchers on the Malaysian Sikh community at various levels, they are more focused on the fields of history, anthropology and sociology with the themes of religion, gender and gurdwara and family institutions. This directly illustrates that social issues are less popular to study scientifically.

There are several studies done specifically on the Sikh community and their socio-cultural and socio-economic issues. One of the major studies, done by Serjit Sahib Singh in 1992, reveals that the community is facing an uphill task in retaining their cultural identity while being surrounded by other bigger and more dominant communities. She also argued that the upcoming generation is weak and vulnerable in terms of culture and religion. Someeta Kaur Sidhu (1996) also agrees that the community is not as strong as a unit. The Sikh people also seem unable to cope with the rapid socio-economic development of the country and feel that the religious teachings are not practical in modern times. The fading of cultural and religious beliefs and practices can lead the younger generation to many social ills. Gurcharan Singh (2013) states that alcoholism is a serious threat for the Sikh community as it causes many families to lose their fathers, brothers and husbands. He mentioned that alcoholism leads to many conflicts and fights, especially after a wedding or sports event. Sarjit and Charanjit Kaur (2008) argue that gurdwara politics is one of the crucial factors that can influence the development of the community. Both argue that the manipulation of power and authority by the Gurdwara Management Committee (GMC) had suppressed the advancement of the community and neglected the lower-income Sikh families. The lack of research on social issues among the Sikh community in Malaysia directly strengthens the general perception that this minority community is numb from problems and does not need the attention of the government to help them, especially from the economic and social aspects.

On the other hand, the study of social issues experienced by the Punjab[6] community has received serious attention among Indian researchers. There are many interesting issues reviewed such as women empowerment, domestic violence, honour killings, alcoholism and many specific studies on drug abuse. Studies on women empowerment show how women raise their status in the economic aspect and strive to achieve financial freedom, which is less popular in a patriarchal society. Dhillon et al. (2007) researched women in different zones of Indian Punjab. They concluded that many women belonging to the age group of 24–56 were involved in farming activities. They can be independent and manage family expenses. Besides, Arora & Arora (2012) studied the perceived impact of microcredit on women empowerment in urban India, with special reference to Punjab, one of the most prosperous states of India. They analyzed that microcredit has a significant impact on the socio-economic status, personality, financial liberation and family relations. Moreover, it was found that women have adapted to the inhibiting factors which are in their stride.

Kumar (2016) examined the determinants of domestic violence among women residing in the rural community of Punjab, India. The study findings show that alcoholic husband, poor education of husband, early marriage, working status of women, and bigger size of the family are more frequently reported factors predisposed to domestic violence. Based on the documented case study and the content analysis methods, Deol (2014) discovered that intolerance of the families to the pre-marital relationships and matrimonial choices of their daughters, especially towards inter-caste marriages, results into the honour killings. The study further observes that in a noticeable number of cases honour killings are executed as crimes of passion aroused by sudden provocation when the couples are caught in compromising situations by the family members of the girls. It has been observed that the centuries-old conformist mindset prevailing in the patriarchal society does not accept the girls to establish pre-marital relations or to find males of their own choices to marry. Hence, Deol (2014) suggested immediate change to the mindset of the bigoted patriarchic societies to become tolerant towards matrimonial choices of their daughters, especially towards inter-caste and inter-religious marriages.

Drinking by college-aged female students in Punjab indicates a pediatric health concern, based on an Trama & Omna (2016) study. Going to the club or disco has become a trend among young girls who get a false sense of liberation and empowerment. The research shows that having male friends increases the risk of alcohol. Kaur & Gill (2015) conducted an experimental study[7] to assess the effectiveness of specific interventions on alcohol use in selected community areas of Punjab. The findings of their study show that specific interventions proved highly effective in reducing alcohol use in selected community areas. In a recent study, Bhullar et al. (2020) discovered that alcohol was the most commonly abused intoxicant by medical students due to different motivational reasons, with a feeling of enjoyment and curiosity leading the causes.

The earliest study on drug abuse was conducted by Lal & Singh (1979) to examine the prevalence and pattern of drug abuse in a rural population of Punjab.[8] Alcohol use was the most common—by 25.55 percent of the sample; a majority of these were occasional or recreational users. Advani (2013) explores the importance of the exceptional aspects of drug abuse among the youth of Punjab, India. According to Verma (2014), 66 percent of the school-going students in the state consume tobacco; every third male and every tenth female student have taken to drugs on one pretext or another and seven out of ten college-going students are into drug abuse. Arora et al. (2017) discovered that the prevalence of substance abuse among the study group was 65.5 percent and most common substance abused was alcohol (41.8 percent), followed by tobacco (21.3 percent). A high prevalence of heroin abusers was noted among study subjects (20.8 percent). The prevalence of non-alcohol and non-tobacco substance abuse was 34.8 percent. A significant association of drug abuse was observed with male gender, illiteracy, and age above 30 years. The Bhullar et al. (2020) study on drug abuse among medical students in Punjab found that a majority of students admitted the fact was not in the knowledge of their parents and that they did not have any regret in experiencing the drug abuse.[9]

METHODOLOGY

Using a Focus Group Discussion (FGD), the researchers used a qualitative methodology for the study. FGD means bringing together people with common backgrounds or perspectives to explore a specific subject of interest. This guided discussion is valuable to gather the ideas, perspectives, opinions and beliefs of individuals on social issues which plagued the Sikh society in both countries. Researchers also initiated the FGD and play a role as moderator and monitor the discussions. All participants were aware of the subject and agreed to be part of the discussion. Thus, the date and time for face-to-face interaction were arranged. Two separate FGDs were conducted and each session lasted about three hours. All respondents are referred to by pseudonyms. Upon completion of the session, the researchers started initial coding by identifying relevant themes. Researchers began to concentrate on coding in which researchers merged some of the codes under a broader framework while removing some of the themes that did not provide many insights. The explanation of why researchers merged certain codes under a broader theme was simply that some of the ideas expressed by the participants were ultimately discovered to be repeated, albeit in different terms. Hence it was important to connect the ideas to a bigger theme (Charmaz, 2006; Krueger, 1994; Ritchie & Spencer, 1994).

FINDINGS AND DISCUSSIONS

In this section, the three main social issues most concerned by the Sikhs are discussed. For the Sikh community in Malaysia, respondents raised the extinction of Punjabi language, while drug abuse is the main concern of the Sikh community in Punjab, India. However, all respondents agreed that alcoholism is the most haunting social issue of the Sikh community around the world.

THEME 1: EXTINCTION OF PUNJABI LANGUAGE IN DAILY INTERACTION

"*Bahasa Jiwa Bangsa*" (Language is the soul of the nationhood) is a popular proverb in Malaysian society, but the complexity of the Punjabi language in the daily interactions among Punjabi Sikhs in Malaysia should indeed be taken seriously. Punjabi language is limited to interactions with the elderly generation and is considered not trendy to speak among friends or relatives. The Sikh community glorifies English more and easily labels someone who is not fluent in English than the mother tongue. Besides, there is also a group of Sikhs who are more comfortable speaking in the national language, Bahasa Melayu, due to exposure to the local community, especially in the neighbourhood and school system.

> I was brought up in a Malay village environment, so we speak mixed the Malay language in every language we know. For example, "Have you *mandi* [bath]?" or "Have you *makan* [eat]?" At one point, I would avoid talking to another Sikh member because of the language barrier. I have an inferiority complex to communicate with them, but I was very happy to go to school because my Bahasa Melayu was better than the Malay friends. Teachers would say, "*Awak ni bukan Melayu macam mana bahasa kamu petah sangat?*" (You're not a Malay, how come you speak so well?) When in secondary school, I picked up Cantonese, Mandarin, Hokkien and even Tamil language. I learned those languages for communication purposes, but I left out my Punjabi language.
>
> (Harnek Singh, 45 years old, Malaysia)

> Very soon the Punjabi language will be forgotten as most families speak English at home and they forget about their language which is Punjabi. Even my kids speak very poorly Punjabi because we did not encourage them. We use to think Bahasa Melayu and English are important in school and Punjabi is not so important. What I read 60 years ago came true when the Punjabi printed newspaper

Malaya Samachar warned that in the next 50 years, the Punjabi language will vanish because of the trend going on now.

(Kuldeep Singh, 62 years old, Malaysia)

The Punjabi language is very essential for Sikhs, but its use which was neglected is picking up now. In Malaysia, conversational Punjabi and written is very minimal, but there is a growing awareness to learn and use it. Government help is needed to keep the teaching of Punjabi growing.

(Jasleen Kaur, 48 years old, Malaysia)

As times are advancing, Punjabi language is diminishing as many youngsters are hooked to social media and tend to speak the social media lingo to be accepted in the fast-moving technology. Many youngsters do not take much interest in learning and practicing Punjabi language. In rural areas, many parents are proud in having their children enrich with the Punjabi language. Many gurdwaras still offer free Punjabi classes to children and constantly encourage them to join these classes. Young children can be seen participating in excitedly in these classes, but this pattern is not observed in the young adults.

(Eykam Kaur, 28 years old, Malaysia)

Among the main causes of the loss of the Punjabi language among the Punjabi ethnic group is due to their status as a minority group in addition to the school system, work environment and neighbourhoods which comprised various cultures of other communities, besides the lack of exposure to the importance of Punjabi language by the Punjabi Sikh community or family themselves.

THEME 2: DRUG ABUSE

Drug abuse is a global social reality affecting almost every country, but its extent and characteristics differ from region to region. Punjab being Sikh population state, the use of tobacco is not favoured or recommended by this community. However, in a survey released by the National Drug Dependence Treatment Centre, AIIMS New Delhi, it was found that the Punjab state discovers its name topping the list with 1.2 lakh children between the ages of 10 and 17 years in the state were alcohol regulars. The study argues that the highest number of alcohol consumers in the country are amongst children—three times more than the national average in the Punjab state (Times of India, 2019).

The misery of drug abuse has developed the proportions of a disease that has shaken the entire society in our Punjab. Our youths are directionless and easily being an influence to take the drug. For some youth, consuming drug and opium is their new lifestyle and "helps" them to cope with the daily struggles. I mean the drug is their medicine for their problems.

(Azad Singh, 65 years old, Punjab)

In my opinion, the problem of drug abuse in the youth of Punjab is a matter of serious concern as every third person is hooked to drugs other than alcohol and tobacco. Changing cultural values, increasing economic strain, and declining supportive and compassionate bonds are leading to beginning into substance use.

(Niral Singh, 28 years old, Punjab)

I am very worried about our Punjabi people in Punjab. Most of them are educated and have good cultural values, but due to poverty, unemployment or family issues, they are more likely to take drugs. Drugs do not solve their problem! The government also does not take this issue seriously. The future of Punjab is not so bright due to such social issues and I think it is now at an alarming level.

(Ikroop Kaur, 44 years old, Punjab)

Drug abuse or substance abuse refers to the use of any intoxicant or psychoactive drug or substance which has a bearing on the physical, mental or psychological health of an individual and families and with a threat to the social and economic fabric of communities and nations. According to the World Health Organization (WHO), substance abuse is persistent or sporadic drug use inconsistent with or unrelated to acceptable medical practice (WHO, 1999). It is a complex phenomenon and Punjab youths may be much more vulnerable to drug or substance abuse. There appear to be several reasons for why Punjab is currently in the midst of a drug epidemic, such as rampaging unemployment, easy and cheap availability of heroin, and the location of Punjab, meaning that most of the drugs will pass through this area on their way to India (Verma, 2014). There is no authentic data available whether a parental educational qualification has any direct bearing on the drug abuse attitude among the youths. However, some drug abuse risk factors can be reduced by parental action which includes poor family management practices, permissive parental attitudes toward adolescent drug abuse, parental drug-using behaviours, high levels of family conflict, low levels of family bonding, peer influence to begin drug use, and the early first use of drugs (Hawkins et al., 1988).

THEME 3: ALCOHOLISM

Respondents from both countries agreed that alcoholism is the gravest social issue among the Sikh.

The consumption of alcohol has become a norm, and one is unable to avoid the invitation to have a drink. As shared by many of the respondents, it is very rare to find a Punjabi man who does not consume alcohol and there is a new tendency of Punjabi females to have a drink at any social events. This behaviour has been widely accepted by the society, although the scripture clearly stated the effect of consuming any kind of intoxicating substance.

> We are not free of problems. I agree that most of our community members are stable in terms of economic income. However, alcoholism is out of control. The men are drinking almost every day. I can't find a function without alcohol and fights.
>
> (Eykam Kaur, 28 years old, Malaysia)

> Alcoholism is a serious issue if you ask me. Is there any party without serving alcohol? Even at my house party, I had to serve alcohol and if I don't serve, I will be cursed by my friends. When we go to people's parties, we nicely consume their beers. But when we don't serve beer in our party, it's a big disrespect.
>
> (Harnek Singh, 45 years old, Malaysia)

Some of the respondents also expressed serious concerns on this issue.

> They should not be drinking at all in the first place. Our religion strongly prohibits consuming alcohol. They deny this fact and drink happily. Sometimes they drink from night until morning. They are proud because they can drink a lot, they feel they are respected because they can be sober even if they drink a lot. This is so sad.
>
> (Meher Kaur, 57 years old, Punjab)

> I agree with this because sadly our community is known as heavy drinkers in this country despite having many positive images. We are known as lawyers, doctors and business people. However, we are also known as drinkers. My friends of other races will always joke with me saying that Bhais (Sikh men)

can drink a lot, that nobody can beat them in drinking. I will just smile at the statement, but in my heart, I feel so embarrassed.

(Eykas Singh, 30 years old, Malaysia)

Yes, I have to agree that drinking is a problem. But I do not see our community as drinking and causing any problems. They drink after work. They silently drink and go back to their houses. Maybe the youngsters who drink irresponsibly are causing problems. The working people drink to release tension after daily heavy work.

(Sanmukh Singh, 38 years old, Malaysia)

The practice of any vices is greatly loathed upon in the Sikh community. Alcoholism does not escape that loathe. The modern families, however, do not see this as an issue. Many families accept the drinking of alcohol, while the conservative families are against alcoholism. Alcohol is still consumed in many Sikh houses during the celebration or in clubs simply because many families do not view alcoholism as a serious issue.

(Tejbir Kaur, 59 years old, Punjab)

The critical views of the respondents clearly show that alcoholism is an important social issue that hampered the Sikh community. Today, the common purpose of consuming alcohol is to get drunk. The impact of globalization and economic liberalization appears to have influenced a widespread attitudinal shift to greater normalization of alcohol use. There is a significant association between increased alcohol consumption and the risk of death from cirrhosis, trauma, and cancer (Kaur & Gill, 2015). On the other hand, most seem immune from attempts by Sikh preachers to press home the view that the faith abhors alcoholism. Parents have a huge role, though it is getting tougher for them with the proliferation of all sorts of movies and cultures now openly available to one and all.

CONCLUSION

As compared to Punjab society, the social issues of the Sikh community in Malaysia have not been carefully studied academically. Despite being known as a committed and dedicated community, they did not miss out on some of the social issues that plagued most Sikh families. The most notable is the poor use of Punjabi among Sikh youths due to the school environment which prioritizes other languages. However, this issue is becoming more chronic as family institutions no longer play an important role in ensuring the survival of this ethnic language. Mastery of the Punjabi language as a basic step towards understanding the text of *Guru Granth Sahib* written in the *Gurmukhi* script. It is observed that in Punjab "drug abuse" is a raging epidemic, especially among the young. Advani (2013) explores the importance of the exceptional aspects of drug abuse among the youth of Punjab, India. From the Advani study, we understand that the rural background of Punjab's drug-user demographic hints at the influence of factors including historical developments in the state's rural economy. Furthermore, it is also related to the Punjabi culture of masculinity, which is deeply tied to images of strength and physical labour. On the other hand, Punjab's Sikh youths' relatively affluent class background suggests that the impact of unemployment and the cultures of consumption and aspiration of modernity associated with injectable drugs are all particularly powerful in driving them to use drugs.

Alternatively, the use of alcohol is very widespread among the Sikhs in both countries. Although the negative effects of alcohol consumption are very obvious, it seems to be a new trend and lifestyle, especially among the youth. Kumar (2016) explains that women with alcoholic husbands and married at an early age were significantly at a greater risk of domestic violence than their counterparts. Interestingly, the female gender is not left behind to achieve "equality" in this aspect. The Trama & Omna (2006) study shows that girls find that alcohol has a disinhibiting effect that enhances their perception of being more confident, increases social comfort and offers feelings of being sexually alluring. In a recent study, Bhullar et al. (2020) discovered that alcohol was the most commonly abused intoxicant by medical students due to different motivational reasons, with the feeling of enjoyment and curiosity leading the causes.

The social problems plaguing the Sikh community should be taken seriously as they occur due to a misunderstanding of Sikh religious principles and ideology. Responsible parties such as the Gurdwara Management Committee (GMC) and non-governmental organizations (NGOs) should be more proactive in addressing these social issues affecting the lives of Sikhs, especially youth. A detailed study with the cooperation of the government is very important so that this issue gets serious attention apart from the need for practical methods to deal with it. At the same time, every Sikh should also be responsible and play their role in line with the philosophy of *Guru Granth Sahib* and the Sikh Code of Conduct (*Sikh Rehat Maryada*).

The government plays an essential role in developing all segments of society, as stated in the Sustainable Development Goals (SDG), "leaving no one behind." The community development policy and strategic plans are needed to manage the social issues among the Sikhs in Malaysia and India. All communities must benefit from the country's economic prosperity to create an advanced economy and inclusive nation. Generally, there is a lack of opportunities for the Sikh minority, especially the youth. Are their problems not important and critical to be brought to the attention of the respective authorities? These problems should be addressed wisely as the Sikhs are also part of the community that will determine the future of Malaysia and India. In a nutshell, the social issues faced by the Sikh community are not being addressed seriously by their respective governments.

REFERENCES

Advani, R. (2013). Factors Driving Drug Abuse in India's Punjab. ISAS Working Paper, No. 177, 24, September, Institute of South Asian Studies (ISAS), National University of Singapore.

Arora, S., & S. Arora. (2012). Role of Micro-Financing in Women Empowerment: An Empirical Study of Urban Punjab. *Pacific Business Review International*, 5(1), 46–60.

Arora, S. B., K. Singh, H. Singh, and P. Kaur. (2017). Drug abuse: Uncovering the burden in rural Punjab. *Journal of Family Medical Primary Care*, 6(1), 558–562.

Brubaker, Rogers. (2006). *Nationalist Politics and Everyday Ethnicity in a Transylvanian Town.* Princeton: Princeton University Press.

Chaturvedi, R. (2010). Review of Pritam Singh, 2008, *Federalism, Nationalism and Development: India and the Punjab Economy. Journal of South Asian Development*, 5(1), 169–172.

Denyer, S. (2013). Drug epidemic grips India's Punjab state. *The Washington Post* [online]. Available from http://articles.washingtonpost.com/2013-01-01/world/36323657_1_afghan-heroin-golden-crescent-pharmaceutical-drugs.

Deol, S. S. (2014). Honour Killings in India: A Study of the Punjab State. *International Research Journal of Social Sciences*, 3(6), 7–16.

Dhillon, M. K., H. Singh & J. Gill. (2007). Involvement of farm women in agricultural and allied activities: factors associated, and constraints faced. *Indian J. Soc. Res.*, 48(3), 221–227.

Duggal, K. S. (1993). *Sikh Gurus: their lives and teachings.* New Delhi: UBS Publishers.

Dusenbery, Verne A. (1997). "Diasporic Imagings and the Conditions of Possibility: Sikhs and the State in Southeast Asia." *Sojourn: Journal of Social Issues in Southeast Asia*, 12(2), 226–60.

Dutta, S. (2012). Green Revolution Revisited: The Contemporary Agrarian Situation in Punjab, India. *Social Change*, 42(2), 229–247.

Gill, Sarjit S. and Charanjit Kaur. (2008). Gurdwara and its politics: Current debate on Sikh identity in Malaysia. *SARI: Jurnal Alam dan Tamadun Melayu*, 26, 243–255.

Gill, Sarjit S. (1999). Diaspora dan masalah identiti Sikh di Malaysia. *Akademika*, 55, 183–192.

Gill, Sarjit S. (2001). Perkahwinan campur peranakan Punjabi di Sabah. *SARI: Jurnal Alam dan Tamadun Melayu 19*: 189–203.

Gullick, J. M. (1953). Captain Speedy of Larut. *JMBRAS, 26*(3), 5–103.

Gurcharan, S. (2012). *Alcohol—a Sikh Social Problem in Malaysia.* Sikh Philosophy Network. Retrieved on 2 November 2013 from http://www.sikhphilosophy.net/people-and-opinion/41428-alcohol-social-disease-many-malaysian-sikhs.html.

Hawkins, David, Richard F. Catalano, and Lori A. Kent. (1991). "Combining Broadcast Media and Parent Education to Prevent Teenage Drug Abuse." In *Persuasive Communication and Drug Abuse Prevention*, ed. Lewis Donohew, Howard E. Sypher, and William J. Bukoski. London: Routledge.

"Home/Census Data 2001/India at a glance." New Delhi: Registrar General & Census Commissioner, India, Ministry of Home Affairs. 2001. Retrieved 8 November 2013.

Kapur, P., & G. Misra. (2003). Image of Self in the Sikh Community: Continuity of the Core and Global Presence. *Psychology Developing Societies, 15*(1), 103–116.

Kumar, R. (2016). Factors associated with domestic violence in a rural community, Punjab India. *International Journal of Advanced Research, 4*(12), 1295–1300.

Kaur, Arunajeet. (2003). The roles of Sikhs in the policing of British Malaya and the Straits Settlements (1874–1957). Master's Thesis, National University of Singapore.

Kaur, B. (2015). Social Impact of Migration in Punjab. *International Journal of Innovative Research & Development, 4*(2), 303–305.

Kaur, C. (2002). *Teks Sikh Rehat Maryada: satu kajian mengenai kod tingkah laku penganut agama Sikh* [Sikh Rehat Maryada Text: A Study of Sikh's Code of Conduct]. Graduation Exercise, Universiti Kebangsaan Malaysia.

Kaur, C. (2012). Komuniti tekstual: peranan Guru Granth Sahib dalam pembentukan identiti gender dalam kalangan lelaki dan perempuan Sikh [Textual community: the role of Guru Granth Sahib in formation of gender identity among Sikh men and women]. Unpublished PhD thesis, Universiti Kebangsaan Malaysia.

Kaur, C. (2017). A textual community: The Sikh minority community in Malaysia. Conference Proceeding International Conference on World Ethnic Minorities' Cultural Heritage and Teaching Innovation (pp. 69–78). Tzu Chi University of Science and Technology, Taiwan.

Kaur, Charanjit. (2003). Perubahan peranan *Granthi* di gurdwara: satu kajian etno-grafi di Kuala Lumpur. Master Project, Universiti Kebangsaan Malaysia.

Kaur, Daljeet. (1986). Ritus Perpeloncoan dalam komuniti Sikh: satu kajian etnografi. Graduation Exercise, Universiti Kebangsaan Malaysia.

Kaur, Daljit. (2000). Gurdwara Sahib Tatt Khalsa dalam sejarah sosial masyarakat Sikh, 1924–1999. Graduation Exercise, Universiti Malaya.

Kaur, Jaswant. (1987). Sikap komuniti Sikh terhadap perkahwinan campur: satu kajian kes di Ipoh, Perak. Graduation Exercise, Universiti Kebangsaan Malaysia.

Kaur, Manchindar. (1992). Gurdwara: satu institusi sosial komuniti Sikh. Graduation Exercise, Universiti Kebangsaan Malaysia.

Kaur, Manjit. (1998). Status dan peranan wanita dalam masyarakat minoriti Sikh di Malaysia: Satu kajian etnografi di institusi gurdwara. Graduation Exercise, Universiti Kebangsaan Malaysia.

Kaur Sidhu, Someeta. (1996). Kebangkitan semula agama Sikh: Satu kajian kes di Kuala Lumpur. Graduation Exercise, Universiti Kebangsaan Malaysia.

Kaur, S. P., and K. Gill. (2015). An Experimental Study to assess the effectiveness of Specific Interventions on Alcohol use in Selected Community Areas of Sangrur, Punjab. *International Journal of Nursing Education*, 7(1), 295–301.

Kaur, Sushila. (1990). First Battalion Perak Sikhs. Graduation Exercise, Universiti Kebangsaan Malaysia

Lal, Brij, & Gurmeet Singh. (1979). Drug abuse in Punjab. *Br J Addict Alcohol Other Drugs*, 74: 411–419.

Malhi, Ranjit Singh. (2015). From Loyal British Subjects to Ardent Revolutionaries: Anti-British Political Activities of the Sikhs in Malaya, 1914–1945. Unpublished PhD Thesis, Asia eUniversity.

Malkiat Singh Dhalliwal & Mukhtiar Kaur Sandhu. (1971). *Some Sikh culture, customs and traditions in Malaya*. Penang: Lopo Ghar.

Manish, S. (2012). What hit this land of plenty? Tehelka [online]. Available from http://archive.tehelka.com/story_main52.asp?filename=Ne140412WHAT.asp.

Nadzan, Haron. (1992). Garrison Taiping 1874–1941. *Malaysia Dari Segi Sejarah*, 20: 38–47.

Patrick, Morrah. (1963). The History of the Malayan Police. *JMBRAS*, 36(2), 5–172.

"Punjab tops list in alcohol consumption among children." Times of India, February 23, 2019.

"Punjab's unemployment rate more than national average." The Tribune, March 7, 2020.

Purewal, Navtej K. (2010). *Son Preference: Sex Selection, Gender and Culture in South Asia*. Oxford: Berg.

Rajuddin, M. R., & J. Kaur. (2010). Faktor-Faktor Yang Mempengaruhi Pembangunan Kaum Sikh Dalam Bidang Keusahawanan di Bandaraya Kuala Lumpur, 1–14.

Sandhu, J. (2004). The Sikh model of the person, suffering, and healing: Implications for counsellors. International Journal for the Advancement of Counselling, 26(1), 33–46.

Sahib Singh, Serjit. (1992). Krisis identiti di kalangan komuniti peranakan Punjabi yangberagama Sikh: satu kajian kes di Pantai Barat Sabah. Graduation Exercise, Universiti Kebangsaan Malaysia.

Sandhu, K. S. (1969). *Indians in Malaya: Some aspects of their immigration and settlement (1786–1957)*. Cambridge: Cambridge University Press.

Sandhu, K. S. (1970). Sikh immigration into Malaya during the period of British rule. In Jerome Ch'en & Nicholas Tarling (eds.). *Studies in the social history of China and South-East Asia*, pp. 335–354. Cambridge: Cambridge University Press.

Sidhu, Manjit S. (1981). Social changes among Sikhs in Peninsular Malaysia. *Malaysia in History*, 24, 49–58.

Simha, V. (2010). Punjab: Rich & Ruined—The Poverty of Plenty, Tehelka [online]. Available from http://archive.tehelka.com/story_main47.asp?filename=Ne021010Cover_story.asp.

Singh, Inder. (1965). *History of Malay States Guides 1873–1919*. Pulau Pinang: Cathay Printers.

Singh, Khushwant. (1966). *A history of the Sikhs II 1839–1964*. New Jersey: Prentice-Hall.

Singh, Pritam. (2008). *Federalism, Nationalism and Development: India and the Punjab Economy*. London: Routledge.

Singh, Sarjit. (1998). Masyarakat minoriti Sikh di Malaysia. Graduation Exercise, Universiti Kebangsaan Malaysia.

Singh, Sarjit. (2001). Kedatangan Orang Sikh dan Penubuhan Gurdwara di Tanah Melayu. *Malaysia Dari Segi Sejarah*, *29*, 31–42.

Singh, Sarjit. (2005). Peranan Gurdwara Dalam Pembentukan Identiti Sikh di Malaysia: Satu Kajian Perbandingan. Unpublished PhD Thesis, Universiti Kebangsaan Malaysia.

Singh, Sukhdave. (1988). Beberapa aspek sosiologi gurdwara di Wilayah Persekutuan. Graduation Exercise, Universiti Malaya.

Singh, S. (2000). Crisis in Punjab Agriculture. *Economic and Political Weekly*, *35*(23), 1891.

Singh, S. (2005). *Political Economy of Contract Farming in India*. Mumbai: Allied Publishers.

Siwar, C., & Y. Kasim. (1997). Urban Development and Urban Poverty in Malaysia. *International Journal of Social Economics*, *24*(12), 1524–1535.

Tatla, Darshan Singh. (1999). *The Sikh Diaspora: The search for statehood*. London: UCL Press.

Taylor, Steve, Manjit Singh & Deborah Booth. (2007). Migration, Development and Inequality: Eastern Punjabi Transnationalism. *Global Networks*, *7*(3), 328–347.

Trama, S., & Omna. (2016). Alcoholism in girls: A theoretical framework. *Indian Journal of Health and Wellbeing*, *7*(12), 1160–1162.

Verma, P. S. (2014). *The Drug Menace: Dimensions, Trends and Tribulations in Punjab*. Chandigarh: Institute for Development and Communication.

Vlieland, C. A. 1932. *British Malaya: A Report on the 1931 Census and Certain Problems of Vital Statistics*. London: Crown Agents.

NOTES

1. Diaspora of Punjabi Sikhs communities exist in Australasia (Bhatti and Dusenbery 2001; McLeod 1986), East Africa (Bhachu 1985; Herzig 2010), North America (Leonard 1996; Mongia 2003), Southeast Asia (Sandhu 1970) and the United Kingdom (Ballard 1982; Bhachu 1991a, 1991b; Singh and Tatla 2006).

2. It is a complete philosophy in itself, not a part of other religions, and independent of other supervision and development. It is a God religion of entire humanity and represents the practice of virtuousness—undivided (sole) and distinctive faith without rituals, exhibitions and disguising (Kaur, 2017, p. 70).

3. As the word of the Forgiving Lord comes to me, so do I express it, O Lalo (*Guru Granth Sahib*, p. 722).

4. The fives symbols are:

Kesh—unshorn/uncut hair, both genders are to keep their *kesh* covered—usually with a turban (headgear) or a scarf.

Kangha—wooden comb placed in hair as symbol of cleanliness.

Kara—steel bracelet as a physical reminder that one is bound to God.

Kachera—cotton underwear (does not always have to be used as underwear) as a reminder to stay away from lust and attachment.

Kirpan—small sword to defend one's faith (self-defense) and protect the weak. Teaches not to seek revenge or retribution but to be free of hatred.

The four prohibitions or mandatory restrictions of the *Khalsa* are:

Not to disturb the natural growth of the hairs.
Not to eat ritually slaughtered meat.
Cohabiting with a person other than one's spouse.
Intoxication (e.g., drugs, tobacco, alcohol and other unhealthful substances).
(Kaur, 2017: 75)

5. For more about the early history of Sikhs, see Inder Singh (1965), Kernial Singh Sandhu (1969, 1970, 1993), Dhalliwal and Sandhu (1971a), Amarjit Kaur (1973), Ranjit Singh Malhi (1977, 2015), Kuldip Singh (1978), Daljeet Kaur (1986), Manjit Singh Sidhu (1991), Manchindar Kaur (1992), Aftar Singh (1993), Manjit Kaur (1998), Sarjit Singh (1998, 2001, 2005), Daljit Kaur (2000), Arunajeet Kaur (2003) and Charanjit Kaur (2002, 2003, 2012, 2018, 2020), Parveen Kaur (2007, 2014), Kiranjit Kaur and Manjit Kaur Ludher (2011). To review the entire bibliography of a study on the Sikh community in Malaysia (1937–2002), refer to Sarjit S. Gill (2002).

6. There are many interesting social issues discussed about the Punjab community, but it is more focused on Pakistan. Therefore, this paper only focuses on the Punjab society in India.

7. Using cluster random sampling technique to recruit 300 males aged between 26 and 55 years to experimental and control groups, the data was collected from five different regions of the district using interview schedule of Alcohol Use Disorder Identification Test (AUDIT). After six months, there was statistically significant ($p < 0.001$) decrease in alcohol use among alcohol users in experimental group, whereas the control group increased their mean alcohol use, which was found to be statistically significant at $p < 0.001$.

8. By a process of systematic random sampling, using the house as a unit, 108 houses with a total of 701 persons were intensively studied. It was found that 29.98 percent of all the persons interviewed had taken drugs at some time in their life. Only four drugs, viz., alcohol, opium, barbiturates and cannabis, were being used.

9. Out of the total 40 students who gave history of drug abuse, a majority of the students, 30 (75 percent), gave history of alcohol abuse, followed by opium at 4 (10 percent) students; tobacco in 3 (7.55 percent) students; cannabis, hallucinogens, sedatives and e-cigarettes by 2 (5 percent) each; and cocaine, amphetamines, heroine, marijuana and other drugs by 1 each (2.5%), with no student showing history of the use of any ecstasy drugs. Drug abuse among medical students is a serious problem and primarily needs to be tackled by medical college authorities.

Chapter 6

Religious Intolerance in India and Malaysia

Benny Thomas Vivian, Sivapalan Selvadurai, Sarjit S. Gill, and Ravichandran Moorthy

INTRODUCTION

India and Malaysia have long been a melting pot of civilizations and cultures, encompassing a wide range of racial, ethnic, and religious groupings. Centuries of interactions between Chinese and Indian traders with the indigenous *Malay* and *Orang Asli* groups of the Malay Archipelago. The subsequent Western colonialism, from the 16th century, created unique plural societies in the Southeast. India is also a multiethnic country with hundreds of tiny ethnic and tribal groupings. This complexity came as a result of a long and extensive history of migration and marriages. Since India is so large and divided into so many states, languages, and religions, its culture is also highly diverse. The rise of multiple societies in Asia and Africa has mostly been the legacy of colonialism. Colonial masters often encourage large-scale migration of their subjects within their colonies, primarily for economic reasons. As these colonies were liberated, many of these ethnic groups remained in their new homes to form plural societies. Pluralism, from an anthropological standpoint, allows for the recognition of ethnic uniqueness and emphasizes variety in society, while also encouraging acceptance and tolerance of those differences. Plural societies commonly exhibit heterogeneous traits from coexisting with other ethnic groups, many of which share the same social and work space. Pluralism also has a political tinge, since it refers to how power and influence are shared in a political process. The relationship between ethnic groups within a society is influenced by how groups strive to maximize their interests due to scarcity of resources and competition for them. Conflict situations may arise when ethnic groups participate in the bargaining process between competing groups (Moorthy 2021).

The de-colonialism process started to take place in the aftermath of the Second World War. The spirit of self-determination and anti-colonialism swept through the colonies, sparking the emergence of nationalism and the struggle for independence. From the 1950s to the 1970s, many countries gained independence. Following the trend of the rest of the world, post-colonial India and Malaysia started working hard to develop and modernize their countries. The formation of a modern state based on a Western nation-state framework and industrial capital structure witnessed the process of socio-political and economic modernization which was foreign to these multicultural Asian developing countries. However, adopting a Western secular approach, in which religion is no longer a relevant political or social force, is seen as incompatible with the way of life of Eastern traditions. Though the political ideals were secular, what transpired during the modernization process was the emergence and prevalence of religion in the public sphere, either by the state or through community life. As a result, aside from ethnic issues and civil conflict, religion's involvement in identity politics, inter-religious interactions, race-relations and ethnicity discourse has become a source of serious concern in many plural societies. Given that race and religion are synonymous in some countries, racial supremacy is similar to religious supremacy, which accelerates the benefit and gain for political parties (Chin 2021). Some scholars suggest that competition and conflict increase the saliency of religious identification and religious diversity, and increase ethnic and religious intolerance (Fox 2004). Religiosity happens to be a carrier as a group identity which is associated with intolerance, but it does not directly cause intolerance (Kunovich & Hodson 1999; Isaacs 2016).

RELIGIOUS REVIVALISM IN INDIA AND MALAYSIA

Malaysia and India have been a beacon of religious pluralism and tolerance in Southeast Asia and South Asia throughout prehistory and even beyond the colonial period. Despite pockets of religious tensions and disputes, these Muslim and Hindu majority countries primarily had stable, progressive, and moderate religious practices that accepted varied cultures, customs, and regional variance. However, this period was short-lived, with both countries experiencing rising inter-ethnic issues due to several state-sanctioned policies deemed discriminatory and marginalist to certain minority groups. Recent events and trends in both countries, however, have indicated a more strong, conservative shift, which has intensified inter-religious conflicts and disagreements. Such incidents of religious intolerance have sparked questions about the underlying currents and causes, as well as the need to deconstruct the nature of the many types of religious intolerance and the role of state institutions. With such a long history of accommodating and tolerating many social groups during colonial and early postcolonial periods, how has religious intolerance become more prevalent in India and Malaysia in recent decades, particularly towards the religious minorities? What went wrong, exactly? These are broad and contextual questions that are investigated in this chapter. This chapter focuses on religious majority actors in the public sphere, namely state/institutional practices that lead to religious intolerance toward religious minorities. The chapter starts with the postulation that democratic majorities have executive power to make decisions on formal state or institutional levels, which may be detrimental to the needs and rights of religious minorities. Ideally, the minorities should be protected under the constitution, and it is the duty of the state to ensure all rights are protected and there are no violations of religious freedoms (i.e., within the bounds of legal regulations).

There are several ethno-religious characteristics that underpin the nature of religious intolerance in these countries. Firstly, both nations are ethnolinguistic and religiously plural societies, with religious minorities from many civilizations and contact zones. Secondly, both countries had British colonial experiences and have evolved from a particular colonial system and experience. Thirdly, though both countries differ in population size, with India's huge 1.2 billion people compared with Malaysia's 33 million people. Fourthly, the majority ethnic group in Malaysia, the *Malays* (also known as the *"son of soil"* or the *Bumiputera*), are of Islamic faith. Their religious civilizational influence comes from the Middle East. This group enjoys special position and rights in the country's constitution owing to their historical and political heritage, which led to the construct of "Malay supremacy" ideology. Furthermore, the late 1970s Islamic revivalism and Islamization process gave rise to the narrative of Malay-Islamic dominance (Neo 2006). Meanwhile, its minority religious groups consisted of Buddhists, Christians and Hindus, predominantly whose forefathers were migrants and diaspora of settled communities. On the other hand, in India, Hinduism is the largest religious group with an indigenous origin. However, the minority groups consisted of Muslims and Christians, all of whom are natives, only that their forefathers converted at some point in time as a consequence of historical conquest and contact during the ruling Mughal Empire followed by British colonialism. Fifth, there is an intriguing interaction, impact, and cultural affinity between India and Malaysia in ethnolinguistic and religious terms. Hinduism, Buddhism, Sikhism, and Jainism all have a specific religious root in India. India's population is likewise indigenous, but religious adherents are indigenous people who have accepted numerous religious traditions from beyond their homeland. Malaysia lacks a native/localized religious origin. Malaysia's population consists mostly of migrant populations that varied in their early and later settlement, as well as a significant number of century-old migrants who have brought their religious customs from their separate homelands.

The Indian polity has been multiethnic, multilingual and multicultural since before the emergence of organized religions. This diversity took place because the lush Ganga belt provided an opportunity for foreign invaders to settle in the rich Indo-Gangetic plain. The highly adaptable *Sanatan Dharma* (the original name of Hinduism), the religion of the land, facilitated the consolidation of people and societies from diverse faith systems and practices. Many other faiths strived and flourished in the Indian polity. The Hindu concept *Vasudeva Kutumbakam* (or world family) had largely facilitated peaceful co-existence in many faiths. Before the arrival of Western powers, India was essentially a religious nation, with several faith systems co-existing. Secularism is a Western construct of governance introduced by the British, especially for post-independence India. Through constitutional revisions, secularism gradually entered into the Indian constitution, politics and governance systems. Secularism is the idea that government and other entities should exist independently of religion or religious beliefs. This concept was foreign to ancient India since the national constitution was created by "cutting and pasting" different constitutions from across the world. However, post-independence India embraced secular characteristics in governance and government structures.

Nevertheless, secularism in India does not totally separate religion and state. The Indian constitution created a secular republic without clear religion-state separation but rather a principled distance between religion and the state (Vaishnav 2019). The Indian constitution has empowered the state to intervene extensively in religious matters, such as the constitutional repeal of untouchability, the opening of all Hindu temples to individuals of lower caste, and so on. The rise of the Bharatiya Janata Party (BJP), a Hindu nationalist political party, since the late 1990s, saw a surge of religious content in the political and social spheres. The BJP's recent electoral comeback has once more highlighted an "alternative nationalism," one founded not on secular ideas but rather on the notion of Indian-Hindu culture, or popularly known as *Hindutva* ideology (Vaishnav 2019). Some scholars claim that it is a populist form of Hindu nationalism which has appealed to the masses in part because it connects meaningfully with everyday anxieties of security, a sense of disorder in modern Indian life. It is a sense of grievance against past injustice coupled with a sense of cultural superiority, an interpretation of history according to this grievance and superiority, a rejection of rational arguments against this interpretation, and an appeal to the majority based on race and masculinity (Chakraborthy 2022).

Malaysian religious revivals were bolstered by both internal and external factors. The global impact of the Iranian Revolution inspired Muslim religious revivals in Malaysia. According to Nagata (1984), during Dr Mahathir Mohamad's (1981–2003) premiership, the state pursued piecemeal Islamization through incentives and measures to counterbalance the challenge posed by Islamist rivals such as the opposition Islamic Party of Malaysia (PAS: Parti Islam SeMalaysia) and independent social movements, particularly the Muslim Youth Movement of Malaysia (ABIM: Angkatan Belia Islam Malaysia), Darul Arqam, and Jamaat Tabligh (in Ahmad Fauzi and Muhamad Takiyuddin 2014).

Islamization policy was aggressively pursued in Malaysia through the institutionalization of Sunni Islam (Mohd Azizuddin 2015). Following the expansion of the Islamic bureaucracy, which included the judiciary, education, and security sectors, came the influence in the private financial services and food sectors. The state's policy of privileging Islam and expanding its role in governance has undermined the secular foundation of the constitution.

The role of institutions in the governance of ethnic religious minorities is important in reducing religious intolerance. On January 29, 2006, the Indian Ministry of Minority Affairs was established to ensure a more focused approach to issues relating to the notified minority communities, which include Muslims, Christians, Buddhists, Sikhs, Parsis, and Jain. The Ministry's mandate includes the development of overall policy and planning, as well as the coordination, evaluation, and review of the regulatory framework and development programmes for the benefit of minority communities. The Ministry's vision is to empower minority communities while also creating an enabling environment for the Indian nation's multiracial, multiethnic, multicultural, multilingual, and multireligious character.

The Malaysian Ministry of National Unity was established in 1972 and then closed down in 1974. The Ministry was reintroduced in 2020 after a long absence, with a vision to lead an inclusive unity for shared prosperity. The Ministry is responsible for managing national unity in a diverse society that practices multiculturalism. The Ministry, however, is not in charge of overseeing ethnic minority issues in Malaysia, such as religious and cultural practices. Some states have an Executive Committee that oversees non-Muslim religious affairs in Malaysia.

RELIGIOUS INTOLERANCE

In reality, religious intolerance, rather than religious diversity, has a role in influencing civil war.(Gomes 2013). Because religious diversity is a common feature of social reality in most multicultural and globalized societies, most studies have focused on religious tolerance; therefore, tolerance has been proposed as a necessary response to the global rise in cultural and religious diversity (Verkuyten et al. 2019; Mishra 2019). Previous study has focused on religious intolerance and discrimination against religious minorities in Western countries, particularly those dominated by Christians. The plight of religious minorities such as Muslims in Christian-majority countries has received much attention. Several attempts were made to compare different religious minorities in the West, but only a few studies were undertaken (Akbaba & Fox 2011). Most comparative studies on religious intolerance have tended to compare Western and Muslim countries (Dangubić et al. 2020; Fox & Akbaba 2015; Akbaba & Fox 2011) but have not addressed differences between Eastern countries in the Asian context, except for Malaysia and Indonesia (Softjan 2016), which happen to be both Muslim majority states. Furthermore, no study has yet to compare religious intolerance between Muslim and Hindu-majority countries. There are a few studies that examine the types of religious intolerance and the role of state-institutions in perpetrating religious intolerance. Further, the susceptibility to class conflict might intensify civil conflict in emerging countries adopting capitalist state systems in the postcolonial period (Kaul 2015). As a result, distinguishing between physical and nonphysical religious intolerance, as well as concentrating on the role of state institutions in religious intolerance, is crucial. In response to this challenge, this chapter examines religious intolerance by state institutions against religious minorities in Muslim-majority Malaysia and Hindu-majority India. This section discusses both physical religious intolerance by state institutions and nonphysical religious tolerance by the state.

Physical Religious Intolerance by State Institutions

Physical religious intolerance involves enforcement by the state authority towards the minority religious groups/organizations/officials that entails arrests and raids, demolishment of religious structures, and restraints on religious symbolisms and attire. Often the state authority enforcement was aided by the majority group's NGOs and resisted by minority groups' NGOs. Three evangelical Christians were detained in Uttar Pradesh, India, on claims of forced conversions against Scheduled Caste/Dalits and intolerance for other religions (Carvalho 2019). The case contains state claims of fostering division or disorder among the various communities (Article 153A of the Indian Penal Code), while the evangelist cited the Bible as a scriptural source to argue for their shared belief and obligation to spread the faith among the people. The right-wing NGO Vishwa Hindu Parishad (VHP), a Hindu Nationalist Organization that strives to prevent Hindus from converting to other religions, was actively monitoring the Schedule Caste/Schedule Tribes.

This right-wing NGO exerted pressure on the state enforcement agency, accusing evangelists of attempting to convert people through incentives and promises of upliftment, as well as portraying them as "attractive and fraudulent" (OpIndia Staff 2019; Carvalho 2019). The VHP supported its "Ghar Wapsi" ("Returning Home") programme of reconverting Hindu caste minority Schedule Caste/Dalits back to Hinduism in response to their conversion to Christianity. The point of contention was whether the state helped or interfered with the VHP reconversion effort. Because of India's secular character, the government should keep out of the initiative. Herein is the distinction between India and Malaysia, both of which profess to be secular and Islamic countries, respectively. Improper proselytism in public spaces is becoming increasingly relevant in a secular ethos, and it is viewed as a sort of incivility. As previously stated, the problem with improper proselytism is that religious groups, particularly proselytizers, put their personal needs and aspirations over the greater good. Questioning others' religious beliefs is socially sensitive at best, and contentious at worst.

Malaysia, on the other hand, has a similar pattern, with authorities raiding Christian minority churches and confiscating religious texts and artifacts believed to be a threat to the majority Islamic religious adherents. For example, in 2011 the Islamic Religious Department of Selangor (JAIS) conducted raids on the Damansara Utama Methodist Church (DUMC) with the assistance of the police (The Star 2011). Harapan Komuniti, a non-governmental organization, used the church centre for an event to recognize its volunteers, leaders, sponsors, and community members who have benefited from its work. However, Datuk Dr. Hasan Ali, a Selangor executive councilor, justified the raid on the church, alleging that there was indications of proselytization toward Muslims (The Star 2011). JAIS is accountable to the Selangor government. JAIS reports directly to the Selangor Sultan (provincial state King), which then rules that the church raid was legitimate. Proselytizing Muslims by members of other faiths is prohibited under Article 11(4), notwithstanding the fact that Muslims themselves may proselytize others (Neo 2014; ICJ 2019). However, the Sultan later took a more moderate position, claiming that there was "insufficient" proof of attempts to convert Muslims to justify legal action, and instead requested that JAIS provide counseling to the Muslims present in the church during the raid (Shazwan 2011).

The religious authority (JAIS) in Malaysia exerts pressure on the King or Sultan, who then consents to JAIS's action. In India, however, it is a religious NGO (VHP) that exerts pressure on the police to act. In both of these cases, the harassment by authorities is mild in comparison to what has been seen in Europe. In India, the majority's insecurity appears to be based on demographic fear, whereas in Malaysia, it appears to be based on Abrahmic religious rivalry. Also, the state's institutional failure on religious issues, as it demonstrates how government bureaucrats are flexing their power over minorities, in addition to unconstitutional actions in response to demands and in violation of the rule of law. Despite the fact that both countries' actions violate minority rights norms, they demonstrate how the state legitimizes political power by using religion as a political instrument to consolidate power and improve the political party position of majority through a cohesive coalition arrangement.

A second mode of physical intolerance entails state enforcement agents' demolition of religious houses of worship belonging to religious minority groups. A century-old holy cross at Bazar road in Bandra was demolished by Brihanmumbai Municipal Corporation (BMC) personnel to reclaim government land from encroachment. The holy cross, which was constructed in or around 1895 and has religious or historical significance, was demolished on private property (Jaisinghani 2017). The holy cross was demolished without due process and despite discussions and dialogue with BMC officials.

In Malaysia, the local council demolished the Sri Maha Mariamman Temple in Padang Jawa, Shah Alam, in a similar manner (The Star 2007). The Malaysian Human Rights Commission (SUHAKAM) is concerned about the trend of desecration of houses of worship in the country (SUHAKAM 2007). According to SUHAKAM, the demolition of places of worship in Malaysia has been carried out mostly due to the fact that some structures were built without the consent of the local authorities, while others were built on government or private land without the permission of the owner. Religious structures, such as Hindu temples, were constructed in rural private plantation grounds, and as urbanization encroached on these areas, they were converted to urban dwellings. This drive to demolish temples under the guise of illegal structures, according to the Hindu Rights Action Force of Malaysia (HINDRAF), was owing to a lack of a transition policy to move these old temple locations, which were deemed sacred by believers. SUHAKAM, on the other hand, feels that the issue should be considered from a broader perspective rather than limited to the legality of occupying land because a place of worship is inextricably tied to one's religion and is recognized as sacred according to one's faith. Local governments and law enforcement personnel should also be more sensitive in their implementation of the legislation, as they may be accused of applying a double standard (SUHAKAM 2007).

Typically, cases involving the demolition of religious structures in both countries demonstrated a lack of adequate policy and sensitivity in dealing with the issues that cause religious intolerance. The government officials' attitude reflects a sense of religious superiority/supremacy disguised as majoritarianism, made possible by the power of political elites to exploit religious nationalism/populism that affects minority groups.

A third form of physical intolerance by state institutions entails restrictions on dress code. In India, the government is likewise attempting to rid educational institutions of all religious symbolism, as is the case in Europe, particularly in France and Belgium, where religious attire (including head scarves) has been banned in schools and public sector jobs since 2004 (FP Explainers 2022; France24 2019; Report on International Religious Freedom 2018). The Karnataka High Court upheld the ban on wearing a hijab/veil at educational institutions in 2022, claiming that it impedes women's empowerment in general and Muslim women in particular (Plumber 2022). In addition, the court noted that hijab is not an essential religious practice in Islam, and that Article 25 of the Constitution guarantees freedom of religion. Malaysia already has restrictions in the civil service for women from wearing sleeveless tops or skirts above knee level (Beh Lih Yi 2018). Also in 2018, guidelines for Muslim women in the private sector were being formulated. Also restrictions for women customers were already in place, where they were barred from government offices for attire that officials deemed as indecent, such as skirts or shorts (Beh Lih Yi 2018). The reasons for dress code restrictions in Malaysia are more focused on portraying and upholding the Islamic identity and modesty, whilst in India it appears to be containing the Islamic identity. In every country, it appears that the majority would prefer that the minority "other" uphold the prevailing ideals or respond by rejecting the "other's" symbolic presence.

Non-physical Religious Intolerance by the State

Non-physical religious intolerance by the state involves enactment of laws restricting minority religious groups. The restrictions entail banning conversion activities, banning usage of religious sacred words, protecting sacred animals and banning unsacred animals deemed sensitive. There is a distinction between the level of restriction placed on the minority religious group based on the cases involved. Several states, including Uttar Pradesh and Himachal Pradesh, Madhya Pradesh, and Jharkhand, have passed anti-conversion laws (Vishwanath 2021; Mander 2017). Minority communities in India's Jharkhand state claimed intolerance as a result of a new anti-conversion law approved by the Jharkhand cabinet (Mander 2017), which went against the secular federal constitution's religious freedom guaranteeing freedom of conscience and the right of all individuals to profess, practice, and propagate religion. The new anti-conversion law imposes harsh prison sentences and fines for evangelizing and converting anyone, particularly married women, children, and the poor, by allurement, coercion, and fraud (Mander 2017; Vishwanath 2021). The BJP-led state Hindu majority government introduced the anti-conversion bill in response to these allegations of unlawful conversion (Pandey 2017;

Vishwanath, 2021). Furthermore, there is a growing fear and insecurity about the Christian population's demographic rise, which increased by 30 percent from 2001 to 2011 (Pandey 2017). According to widespread opinion, the rise of religious nationalism/populism in India has resulted in an increase in anti-conversion legislation in several states (Sahgal et al. 2021). However, a more nuanced understanding of the laws is not about proselytism/conversion per se, but rather contesting what constitutes improper proselytism or unlawful conversion in light of proselytizers' and targets' rights, as well as the state's interests (Hertzberg 2020; Vishwanath 2021). To begin with, evangelical Christians contend that the legislation infringes on their fundamental right to propagate, limiting their religious freedom to practice/manifest their faith (Hertzberg 2020). However, when Hindus reacted by converting individuals who had been converted through the homecoming programme Ghar Wapsi, there was a protest (Venugopal 2015). Second, Hindus argue that forced and enticing missionary attempts infringe on the right of the target to practice their religion. Hindus, who do not proselytize, are afraid of a demographic backlash, as well as believing in a worldview of seekers of truth/god, as opposed to Abrahamic believers of truth/god (Venugopal 2015). Third, in order to maintain public order, the state frequently protects dominant religious traditions (Hertzberg 2020).

However, in Malaysia, the state permitting conversion of minorities has become an intolerance issue. Unilateral conversion of children by one parent who has embraced majoritarian Islam, without the consent of the minority other (Siang 2012), leads to custody disputes and subsequent disruption of family. Literal interpretation of "parent" as singular in the Federal constitution has favored the majoritarian religious group (Siang 2012). Unilateral conversion is viewed as unjust, as consent must be obtained from both parents prior to the conversion of their children. Issues of equality between the parents of different religions as well as parental right over the religion of a child who is born before one of his or her parents converts to Islam were contested.

The opposing views of India and Malaysia on conversion and how it affects intolerance toward minorities are based on two different majoritarian worldviews. The Indian state, with a majority non-proselytizing religion (or sanatana dharma), restricts conversion because it considers conversion to be improper proselytising and minorities' fear of population growth, as well as upholding Hindutva ideology. While the state of Malaysia actively promotes the majority faith for conversion out of a favorable interest and in accordance with the Islamic state's aspiration.

The second restriction entails the banning usage of religious sacred words. For example, since 1986, an administrative order from the Malaysian Home Ministry prohibits the use of the term "*Allah*" in Christian publications on the grounds of public order and prevention of misunderstanding between Muslims and Christians (CFM 2011). In 2010, the Catholic church challenged the ministerial order in regard to the word *"Allah"* used by the Catholic church in their Malay language publication in a weekly newsletter. The high court then decided in favor of the church in 2010, but its decision was overturned on appeal in 2013 (Neo 2014). The *"Allah"* case also triggered physical intolerance from government enforcement at the federal and state levels where Bibles in the Malay language and material such as CDs have been seized by the authorities. The government stance is based on the provision of Article 11(5), which prohibits acts deemed to affect public order (i.e., sensitivity of the majority) (Neo 2014).

According to the minority Christians, being denied the use of the word *"Allah"* in Malay disregards the constitutional right of Malaysian citizens to freedom of religion under the Federal Constitution. Article 11 safeguards the right of each Malaysian to profess and practice one's religion of choice and Article 11(3) expressly provides that every religious group has the right to manage their own religious affairs (Nurhalida 2014). There are several reasons that can be attributed to state's stance on the *"Allah"* issue, namely tribal and territorial use due to tradition (Fuller 2014), the presence of a Malay language bible in the region, supremacist and exclusivist thinking, insecurity or fear of deception and confusion, Abrahamic rivalry in proselytizing (Neo 2014), its classification in secrecy (Lim 2017) and its use as a political tool to beef up support for the ruling party (The Guardian 2014).

A third type of nonphysical state intolerance involves protecting the sacred animal cow, considered to be holy by many Hindus, or resisting non-sacred animals that were deemed sensitive by the majority religious group. The ruling BJP government in May 2017 banned the sale of cattle for slaughter and restricted cattle trade to farm owners (Sinha 2017) before India's Supreme Court suspended a government ban on the trade of cattle for slaughter in July 2017 (Rajalakshmi 2018). The meat and leather sellers, who were primarily Muslim, were the hardest hit by the law and also faced community prejudice, including escalating violence from increasingly forceful cow vigilante organizations (Chauhan 2017). The Union Ministry of Environment, Forests and Climate Change (MoEFCC) has been notified the new rules under the Prevention of Cruelty to Animals Act, which bans the sale of cattle for slaughter in open markets across the country (Shekhar and Parashar, 2017). These rules had a huge negative impact on some states such as the state of Kerala, where around 60 percent of the total meat consumed is beef. Not just Muslims and Christians, but some Hindus in northeast Indian states also consume beef. Since the BJP came to power in 2014, some states, including Haryana, have passed stringent rules prohibiting cow slaughter (Babu 2017). However, anti-slaughter laws in several Indian states violate Muslims' religious freedom to sacrifice a cow on the Islamic holy day of *Bakra Eid* (*Eid al-Adha*) and would exacerbate religious intolerance against minority religious groups. In addition, the state of Karnataka resumed efforts in December 2020 to pass a bill banning cow slaughter in the state after the bill failed to pass in the upper house of the legislature, where the ruling BJP does not have a majority (Babu 2020).

While in Malaysia, restrictions and bans on religious minorities' activities followed a similar pattern, with the Muslim NGO Solidarity and Charity Organisation (ISCO) requesting that the Penang Municipal Council (MPPP) prohibit the open sale of pork in George Town, as the activity was perceived as being insensitive to Muslims (The Edge 2014). Non-Muslims selling pork openly was not a problem in the state of Kelantan, which was administered by the Islamic Party of Malaysia (PAS) (The Edge 2014). This shows that when a regional state is dominated by a strong majority of one religious group, as in Kelantan, it looks to be more tolerant, and when the religious majority's population is smaller, as in Penang, it appears to be less tolerant. Is this stance due to the religious majority's desire to exercise power or suggest some sort of entitlement, or to the religious minority's need to respect the religious majority's sensitivities in the community? Because there is no specific regulation prohibiting the sale of pork in the open-air market, the city council has the authority to order the pig vendors to close down if a complaint is received from the majority Muslim community. It demonstrates the majority Muslim's predominance over non-Muslim minorities.

In comparison, both countries enacted legislation restricting and prohibiting the activities of minority religious groups. Both countries, however, have varying levels of nonphysical intolerance, with India's laws enacted in response to physical action by the majority communal groups. While in Malaysia, the rule prohibiting the use of the sacred word *"Allah"* in Malay in the bible is considered non-essential to minority Christians and claimed by the state to belong only to the majority Muslim, and is seen as territorial and tribal in nature. Meanwhile, India's state rule banning slaughter of sacred cows and Malaysia's banning of unsacred pork suggest a violation of multicultural public space that also interferes with private consumption. Cows became a sacred symbol of the nationalist movement during the colonial period, uniting Hindus from all classes, castes, and regions against the British. Today, the symbol is being used to bring Hindus from all walks of life together. The difference this time is that it is members of the ruling party who are fueling and even inciting hatred towards India's Muslims, who are seen as a threat and as outsiders (Jain 2019). In both countries, majoritarianism is predominant, which imposes its values and norms and is intolerant of minority sensitivities.

DISCUSSION AND CONCLUSION

Religious intolerance in the Western world appears to be focused on defending secular ideals, particularly rejecting the penetration of religious symbols (veil, cross, etc.) into the public sphere. Whereas in Malaysia and India, religious values are preserved through the sacredness of religious symbols (words like "*Allah*," animals like cows) where such symbols are prohibited on minorities in public. An exception is the Indian experience of religious intolerance toward *purdah* (veil) in educational institutions, which appears to follow the Western secular path.

Both countries experience religious revivalism, in the early 1980s Islamisation process in Malaysia impacted bureaucratic, financial, and public spaces, while in India in the early 2010s, witnessed the Hindutva religious fervor. The more aware you are of your religious beliefs, the more divisive you become, reducing contact with other religious people, resulting in greater stereotypes and prejudices with attending social identity, which can lead to religious intolerance. With religion occupied in the public sphere and ethnic-based politics since independence have triggered tension between the ethno-religious communities. The rise in religious consciousness has been attributed to the growing global revival; others have related it to the state's strategy of maintaining its ethnic identity in the face of minority assertiveness in both the economic and social sense. Political parties have taken advantage of the revival to establish an identity that attributes to the exclusivity of the majority in order to fight the religious sentiment and occasionally construct a narrative of religious conflict between the majority and minority.

Religion was used in India in response to the external threat of Abrahamic religion spread/diffusion in India and the threat of modernity. Ironically, the minority Muslims used secularism to claim religious discrimination in public spaces, despite the fact that questionable practices continue to exist. In Malaysia, the situation is slightly different, with a reversal of the trend. Religion was used to pacify internal threats/security where attempts were made to consolidate majority power by bringing diverse political parties and ideologies of the majority group together. The non-Muslim minority used secularism to claim injustice, whereas the majority group used the religious state as a route to consolidate power. Herein lies the contradiction: the Muslim minority seeks justice through public-sphere secularism, as in India, while the Muslim majority rejects secularism as a model, as in Malaysia.

According to social identity theory, when a social group's standing is threatened or diminished, members' self-esteem can be undermined, fostering intolerance and resulting intergroup conflict (Milligan 2012). The Christian proselytizing and conversion efforts in India rendered the Hindu majority to feel threatened and vulnerable. Similarly, Muslims' zeal for religious expression through purdah, mosque sounds, and religious adherence made Hindus feel insecure. Both of these groups, being Abrahamic and missionary, bear negative group stereotypes that tend to lower the self-esteem of the majority of Hindus, who then respond intolerantly through state institutions.

A similar argument may be made for the Muslim majority in Malaysia, who see Christian missionary work as a threat and seek to restrict it through the support of the majority's religious bodies and rulers. Another plausible argument for the intolerance is that the majority masses are more inclined to feel vulnerable to minorities if they have less economic security. The implication is that the majority, with job market insecurity and lower economic status (i.e., B40 group), is more inclined to seek state support, which is often intolerant of people of different faiths. As such, religious intolerance is determined by both structural political economic interests and social identity.

Tolerance of religious diversity in a plural society is a social reality that the majority should cultivate rather than impose their sacred symbols on minorities, such as prohibiting the use of the phrase "*Allah*," halal food in public spaces, and restrictions on "cow slaughter." The majority should accept other cultures and refrain from forcing their ideals on others, resulting in a more respectful interaction between religious groups. Conflicting religious worldviews co-existing peacefully and a culture of religious tolerance can foster societal unity, which is critical for political stability. It takes a political will for majority authorities to defend minorities as a true responsibility to uphold the constitution that protects the whole citizen.

Another noteworthy concern is the possibility of nonphysical religious intolerance progressing to physical intolerance. As such, we cannot ignore the potential for the state's nonphysical religious intolerance to be emulated by communal and other social organizations, resulting in further division and even encountering physical intolerance.

REFERENCES

Ahmad, Fauzi, Abdul Hamid, & Muhamad Takiyuddin Ismail. 2014. "Islamic Conservatism and the Demise of Islam Hadhari in Malaysia." *Islam and Christian-Muslim Relations* 25(2): 159–180.

Akbaba, Yasemin, & Jonathan Fox. 2011. "Religious Discrimination against Muslim Minorities in Christian Majority Countries: A Unique Case?" *Politics, Religion & Ideology* 12:4, 449–470. http://dx.doi.org/10.1080/21567689.2011.624414

Babu, Ramesh. 2017. "Centre's notification banning cow sale for slaughter a fascist move: Kerala." *Hindustan Times*, July 19, 2017. https://www.hindustantimes.com

/india-news/centre-s-notification-banning-cow-sale-for-slaughter-a-fascist-move
-kerala/story-rLcy0LV3hh44H7TxwU0ZYJ.html

Babu, Venkatesha. 2020. "Karnataka cabinet passes ordinance to ban cow slaughter
in state." *Hindustan Times*, December 28, 2020. https://www.hindustantimes.com
/india-news/karnataka-cabinet-passes-ordinance-to-ban-cow-slaughter-in-state/
story-JiY4mdaxsDxdZTtauoddxO.html

Beh Lih Yi, 2018. "Malaysia told to stop 'policing' women's clothing with dress
code plan." *Reuters*, August 9, 2018. https://www.reuters.com/article/us-malaysia
-women-idUSKBN1KT227

Carvalho, Nirmala. 2019. "Uttar Pradesh, three evangelical Christians arrested for
'forced conversions.'" *Asianews*, November 11, 2019. https://www.asianews
.it/news-en/Uttar-Pradesh,-three-evangelical-Christians-arrested-for-forced
-conversions-48678.html

Chakraborthy, Antara. 2022. "Hindutva's Rise and Social Cohesion: Ponder the
Improbable." *S. Rajaratnam School of International Studies (RSIS)*, February
8, 2022. https://www.rsis.edu.sg/rsis-publication/cens/hindutvas-rise-and-social
-cohesion/#.Yn-q5ehBzIU

Chauhan, Chetan. 2017. "Centre bans sale of cows for slaughter at animal markets,
restricts cattle trade." *Hindustan Times*, July 19, 2017. https://www.hindustantimes
.com/india-news/centre-bans-cow-slaughter-across-india-cows-can-be-sold-only
-to-farmers/story-8sFXJxiNmZ8eD6NXDgbvnL.html

Kuek, Chee Ying, and Tay Eng Siang. 2012. "Unilateral Conversion of a Child's
Religion and Parental Rights in Malaysia." *Singapore Academy of Law Journal*
24(1): 92–112.

Chin, James. 2021. "Malaysia: identity politics, the rise of political Islam and
Ketuanan Melayu Islam," in *Religion and Identity Politics: Global Trends and
Local Realities*, edited by Mathews Mathew and Melvin Tay, 75–95. Singapore:
World Scientific.

Christian Federation of Malaysia (CFM). 2011 "10-Point Solution Ad Hoc And Short
Term Resolution." *National Evangelical Christian Fellowship*. https://www.necf
.org.my/newsmaster.cfm?&menuid=43&action=view&retrieveid=1288

Dangubić, M., M. Verkuyten & T. H. Stark. 2020." Rejecting Muslim or Christian
religious practices in five West European countries: a case of discriminatory rejection? " *Ethnic and Racial Studies* 43(16): 306–326.

Fox, Jonathan, & Yasemin Akbaba. 2015. "Securitization of Islam and Religious
Discrimination: Religious Minorities in Western Democracies, 1990–2008."
Comparative European Politics 13:175–197.

Fox, Jonathan. 2004. "The Rise of Religious Nationalism and Conflict:Ethnic Conflict
and Revolutionary Wars, 1945–2001." *Journal of Peace, Research* 41(6):715–731.

FP Explainers. 2022. "Hijab ban stays in Karnataka: A look at countries where veils
are barred." *First post*, March 15, 2022. https://www.firstpost.com/world/hijab-ban
-stays-in-karnataka-a-look-at-countries-where-veils-are-barred-10460931.html

France 24. 2019. "French move to extend ban on religious symbols sparks
fears of 'radical' secularism." *France24*, October 31, 2019. https://uk.news
.yahoo.com/french-move-extend-ban-wearing-200000252.html?guccounter=1

&guce_referrer=aHR0cHM6Ly93d3cuZ29vZ2xlLmNvbS88&guce_referrer_sig
=AQAAAB96GMqW6c2TWecyd-9s-arVhrqkPXJRviMO6wPWQWbXu7aCsKj7
ljwQJ8YpR9bvlXIhhogPKEYrTGAlfnlxJ04JmicgPOUm_7Fu8qMceimdFmMZp
HgLO6o3Sc1wHNGPXLdguzHN2DWrezOm-qB5oGjmua2BE2NLfgGerbsP7by3

Fuller, Thomas. 2014. "The Right to Say 'God' Divides a Diverse Nation." *The New York Times*, November 3, 2014. https://www.nytimes.com/2014/11/04/world/asia/in-malaysia-allah-is-reserved-for-muslims-only.html

Gomes, Joseph Flavian. 2013. "Religious diversity, intolerance and civil conflict." Universidad Carlos III De Madrid Working Papers. Economics Paper 13–11, Calle Madrid. Departamento de Economía. https://e-archivo.uc3m.es/bitstream/handle/10016/17122/we1311.pdf?sequence=1

Hertzberg, Michael. 2020. "The gifts of allurement: anti-conversion legislation, gift-giving, and political allegiance in South Asia." *Journal of Contemporary Religion* 35(1): 93–114.

International Commission of Jurist (ICJ). 2019. "Challenges to Freedom of Religion or Belief in Malaysia A Briefing Paper." *International Commission of Jurists*. https://www.icj.org/wp-content/uploads/2019/03/Malaysia-Freedom-of-religion-brief-Advocacy-Analysis-brief-2019-ENG.pdf

Isaacs, Matthew. 2016. "Faith in Contention: Explaining the Salience of Religion in Ethnic Conflict." *Comparative Political Studies* 50(2): 200–231. https://doi.org/10.1177/0010414016655534

Jain, Kalpana. 2019. "Cow Vigilantes and the Rise of Hindu Nationalism." Kennedy School Review. A Harvard Kennedy School Student Publication, May 3, 2019. https://ksr.hkspublications.org/2019/05/03/cow-vigilantes-and-the-rise-of-hindu-nationalism/

Jaisinghani, Bella. 2017. "Christians to go to court against razing of cross." *Times of India*, May 1, 2017. https://www.timesofindia.indiatimes.com/city/mumbai/christians-to-go-to-court-against-razing-of-cross/articleshow/58450649.cms

Kaul, Nitasha. 2015. "On Hindutva hate politics: A few things I wasn't able to discuss with Ram Madhav on Al Jazeera." *Scroll.in,* December 30, 2015. https://www.scroll.in/article/778661/a-few-things-i-wasnt-able-to-discuss-with-bjp-leader-ram-madhav-during-his-al-jazeera-interview.

Kunovich, Robert M., and Randy Hodson. 1999. "Conflict, Religious Identity, and Ethnic Intolerance in Croatia." *Social Forces* 78(2): 643–674.

Lim, Ida. 2017. "Court refuses church's bid, says govt's reasons for 'Allah' ban classified under OSA." *malaymail*, October 16, 2017. https://www.malaymail.com/news/malaysia/2017/10/16/court-refuses-churchs-bid-says-govts-reasons-for-allah-ban-classified-under/1488241

Mander, Harsh. 2017. "Why Jharkhand's anti-conversion bill is against Constitution and not necessary." *Hindustan Times*, September 12, 2017. https://www.hindustantimes.com/columns/why-jharkhand-s-anti-conversion-bill-is-against-constitution-and-not-necessary/story-FIhGsnxuqIItvniVAoiLQO.html

Milligan, Scott. 2012. "Economic inequality, poverty, and tolerance: Evidence from 22 countries." *Comparative Sociology* 11(4): 594–619.

Mishra, Vibha. 2019. "Religion and Globalization." *International Scientific Refereed Research Journal* 2(1): 25–28.

Mohd Azizuddin Mohd Sani. 2015. Islamization Policy and Islamic Bureaucracy in Malaysia. Singapore: Institute of Southeast Asian Studies. ISEAS Publishing.

Moorthy, Ravichandran. 2021. "Hybridity and Ethnic Invisibility of the Chitty Heritage Community of Melaka." *Heritage* 4(2): 554–566. https://doi.org/10.3390 /heritage4020033

Nagata, Judith. 1984. *The Reflowering of Malaysian Islam: Modern Religious Radicals and Their Roots*. University of British Columbia Press.

Neo, Jaclyn Ling-Chien. 2006. "Malay Nationalism, Islamic Supremacy and the Constitutional Bargain in the Multi-Ethnic Composition of Malaysia." *International Journal on Minority and Group Rights* 13(1): 95–118.

Neo, Jaclyn Ling-Chien. 2014. "What's in a name? Malaysia's 'Allah' controversy and the judicial intertwining of Islam with ethnic identity." *International Journal of Constitutional Law* 12(3): 751–768. https://www.researchgate.net/publication /278326758_What%27s_in_a_name_Malaysia%27sAllah_controversy_and_the _judicial_intertwining_of_Islam_with_ethnic_identity

Nurhalida, Mohamed Khalil. 2014. "Parameters of freedom of religion." *New Straits Times*, December 11, 2014. https://www.nst.com.my/news/2015/09/parameters -freedom-religion

OpIndia Staff. 2019. "UP: Christian Missionaries with Hindu names organised 'Dharmasabha' to convert sick people to Christianity, arrested." November 27, 2019. https://www.opindia.com/2019/11/uttar-pradesh-padre-conversion -christianity-arrested/

Pandey, Prashant. 2017. "Jharkhand passes anti-conversion Bill, govt rejects demand for more scrutiny." *The Indian Express*, August 13, 2017. https://indianexpress.com /article/india/jharkhand-passes-anti-conversion-bill-govt-rejects-demand-for-more -scrutiny-4794360/

Plumber, Mustafa. 2022. "Hijab Ban-Insistence On Wearing Purdah, Veil Or Headgear In Any Community May Hinder Emancipation Of Women: Karnataka High Court." *LiveLaw.in*, March 15, 2022. https://www.livelaw.in/top-stories/ hijab-ban-insistence-on-wearing-purdah-veil-or-headgear-in-any-community-may -hinder-emancipation-of-women-karnataka-high-court-194232

Rajalakshmi, S. 2018. "Supreme Court suspends ban on cattle trade for slaughter." *The Hindu Business Line*, January 11, 2018. https://www.thehindubusinessline.com /news/supreme-court-suspends-ban-on-cattle-trade-for-slaughter/article64271552 .ece

Report on International Religious Freedom, 2018: "Belgium." https://www.state.gov/ reports/2018-report-on-international-religious-freedom/belgium/

Sahgal, Neha, Jonathan Evans, Ariana Monique Salazar, Kelsey Jo Starr and Manolo Corichi. 2021. "Religion in India: Tolerance and Segregation." *Pew Research Center*, June 29, 2021. https://www.pewresearch.org/religion/2021/06/29/religion -in-india-tolerance-and-segregatio/

Shazwan, Mustafa Kamal. 2011. "Selangor Sultan Backs Jais Church Raid, No One To Be Charged." *Malaysia Today*, October 10, 2011. https://www.malaysia-today.net/2011/10/10/selangor-sultan-backs-jais-church-raid-no-one-to-be-charged/

Shekhar, Praveen, and Reema Parashar. 2017. "Government bans sale of cows for slaughter at cattle markets, restricts trade." *IndiaToday (New Delhi)*, July 11, 2017. https://www.indiatoday.in/india/story/sale-of-cattle-for-slaughter-banned-at-markets-across-the-country-environment-ministry-979388-2017-05-26

Sinha, Bhadra. 2017. "Cattle trade for slaughter: Supreme Court suspends ban across India." *Hindustan Times (New Delhi)*, July 12, 2017. https://www.hindustantimes.com/india-news/supreme-court-puts-on-hold-ban-on-cattle-trade-for-slaughter-govt-says-new-rules-by-august-end/story WypElt9CMgFZP1wxPsLdgJ.html

Softjan, Dicky. 2016. "Religious Diversity and Politico-Religious Intolerance in Indonesia and Malaysia." *The Review of Faith & International Affairs* 14(4): 53–64.

SUHAKAM. 2007. "Demolition Of Places Of Worship." Annual Report 2007 Human Rights Commission of Malaysia. 2007. https://www.suhakam.org.my/wp-content/uploads/2013/11/ar2007.pdf

The Edge. 2014. "#Highlight* Muslim NGO: Prohibit traders from selling pork openly." *The Edge (Malaysia)*, January 24, 2014. https://www.theedgemarkets.com/article/highlight-muslim-ngo-prohibit-traders-selling-pork-openly-1

The Guardian, 2014. "Malaysia censors Ultraman comic for 'irresponsible use of the word Allah.'" https://www.theguardian.com/world/2014/mar/07/malaysia-censors-ultraman-comic-allah

The Star. 2011. "Hasan claims event was to proselytize Muslims." *The Star News*, August 5, 2011. https://www.thestar.com.my/news/nation/2011/08/05/hasan-claims-event-was-to-proselytise-muslims

The Star. 2007. "Samy: Talk first before demolishing temples." *The Star News*, November 3, 2007. https://www.thestar.com.my/news/nation/2007/11/02/samy-talk-first-before-demolishing-temples

Vaishnav, Milan. 2019. Religious nationalism and India's future. The BJP in power: Indian democracy and religious nationalism. Carnegie Endowment for International Peace. https://carnegieendowment.org/2019/04/04/religious-nationalism-and-india-s-future-pub-78703

Venugopal, Vasudha. 2015. "Hindus are seekers, not believers: Ghar Wapsi not in our ethos, says spiritualist Jaggi Vasudev." *The Economic Times*, March 27, 2015. https://economictimes.indiatimes.com/opinion/interviews/hindus-are-seekers-not-believers-ghar-wapsi-not-in-our-ethos-says-spiritualist-jaggi-vasudev/articleshow/46709506.cms?utm_source=contentofinterest&utm_medium=text&utm_campaign=cppst

Verkuyten, Maykel, Kumar Yogeeswaran and Levi Adelman. 2019. "Intergroup Toleration and Its Implications for Culturally Diverse Societies." *Social Issues Policy Review* 13(1): 5–35.

Vishwanath, Apurva. 2021. "3 states, 3 anti-conversion laws: what's similar, what's different." *The Indian Express*, January 3, 2021. https://indianexpress.com/article/explained/religion-conversion-bill-bjp-7129285/

Index

About the Contributors

EDITORS

Ravichandran Moorthy, Ph.D., is Associate Professor of International Relations and the Head of the Post-Graduate Programme at the Research Centre for History, Politics and International Affairs, Faculty of Social Sciences and Humanities, Universiti Kebangsaan Malaysia. He teaches and conducts research in international relations, security studies and bioethics, with a special focus on ASEAN and South Asian affairs. He has numerous academic publications to his name, including three edited volumes and several papers in highly cited journals. His works have appeared in high-impact journals like the *Asian Survey*, *International Relations of the Asia Pacific*, *Sustainability*, *Water Policy* and *Journal of Palm Oil Research*. His three edited books cover the topics of Resource Politics, Sustainable Governance, and Conflict Resolution. Dr. Ravichandran is very active in the bioethics fraternity in the Asia Pacific, and he currently serves as the president of the Asian Bioethics Association. Dr. Ravichandran has also served as a consultant for a number of organizations, including the Institute of Diplomatic Studies, the Ministry of Foreign Affairs, Timor Leste, UNESCO Bangkok, the South Korean Embassy, and a number of Malaysian government institutions. He has extensive networking with many agencies around the Asia Pacific, and has been invited as Keynote Speaker at numerous seminars and conferences around the world.

Sarjit S. Gill, Ph.D., is a Professor of Social Anthropology and the former Head of the Department of Social and Development Sciences, Faculty of Human Ecology, Universiti Putra Malaysia. His current research interests include Malaysian ethnic relations and minority studies. Prof. Sarjit has been referred to by several ministries, agencies, local communities, and special interest groups. He is a member of the Malaysian Institute of Integrity and a former Executive Editor for the *Malaysian Journal of Youth Studies*,

121

the Malaysian Youth Development Research Institute (IYRES), Ministry of Youth and Sports. He was a Guest Writer for the Ministry of Higher Education and a member of the Task Force to review SUHAKAM's *Report of National Inquiry into Indigenous Peoples' Land Rights in Malaysia*. Prof. Sarjit is currently a member of the Malaysian History Textbook Advisory Panel, Ministry of Education Malaysia. He has represented Malaysia in three important international engagements, namely the Peace and Human Security Workshop organized by UNESCO in Bangkok, Thailand (2007), the Interfaith Conference in Perth, Australia (2009), and the Interfaith Summit in Bali, Indonesia (2012).

CONTRIBUTORS

Suseela Devi Chandran, Ph.D., is Associate Professor of International Relations at Faculty of Administrative Science and Policy Studies, UiTM, Shah Alam. She teaches and researches on issues related to Asia Pacific security, ASEAN and Malaysia–India bilateral relations. While teaching in UiTM, she also teaches the Education in Human Values (EHV) program under the auspices of a non-governmental organization, namely Sathya Sai International Organization Malaysia (SSIOM).

Angelina Gurunathan is an Administrative and Diplomatic Officer with the Malaysian Government pursuing her doctorate in Strategic and Security Studies at the National University of Malaysia (UKM). Prior to her sabbatical, she served at the Ministry of International Trade and Industry for nearly 14 years and her area of interest is the economic and security nexus of emerging economies, with a particular focus on India and ASEAN.

Charanjit Kaur, Ph.D. (National University of Malaysia), is an Assistant Professor in the Department of General Studies at Universiti Tunku Abdul Rahman's Faculty of Creative Industries (UTAR). Her area of study is cultural anthropology, with a focus on Malaysia's Sikh minority group, where she analyzes themes such as religious-cultural conflict, gender identity, and social behavior. The majority of her research findings have been published as book chapters as well as in local and international periodicals. She has delivered keynote addresses at numerous international and regional conferences, forums, and seminars. She is also frequently invited as a member of the Sikh religious panelist and field expert in various academic and community forums organized by Malaysian agencies and non-governmental organizations (NGOs), local and private universities, and religious bodies such as

Institut Darul Ehsan (IDE), Institut Integriti Malaysia (IIM), TV Alhijrah, Global Unity Network, TV2 Fresh Brew, and Radio Traxxfm.

Tharishini Krishnan, Ph.D., is a Senior Lecturer of Strategic and Defence Studies, Faculty of Defence Studies and Management at the National Defence University Malaysia. She teaches and researches on issues of Indo Pacific, Indian Ocean, South Asia, Maritime Security and Naval Strategy. Her works have appeared in the *Diplomat*, Asia Maritime Transparency Initiative, East Asia Forum, Policy Forum and *Journal of Asian Economic Integration*. She is the current Head of Department of Strategic and Defence Studies and Visiting Fellow to the Malaysia-Australia Maritime Virtual Exchange Program.

K. Puvaneswaran, Ph.D., is a Senior Lecturer at the Department of Social and Developmental Sciences, Universiti Putra Malaysia. He obtained his Ph.D. in the field of Community Development and Tourism from the University Putra Malaysia. His research mainly focused on community-based tourism, indigenous tourism, sustainable tourism practices and cultural tourism studies. He has delivered keynote speeches in various countries, including China and India, on contemporary issues of sustainable tourism. He is also the Honorary Treasurer of the ASEAN Tourism Researchers Association (ATRA), Associate Director of the Center of Research and Innovation in Tourism, and a Visiting Professor at Lyceum of the Philippines University (LPU).

K. S. Nathan, Ph.D., is a Visiting Research Fellow in the Institute of Ethnic Studies (KITA), Universiti Kebangsaan Malaysia, Bangi. He also holds LL.B and LL.M degrees from the University of London. He is also the current President of the Malaysian Association for American Studies (MAAS). He was Professor of International Relations in the Faculty of Social Sciences, University of Malaya, Kuala Lumpur from 1994 to 2001, Senior Fellow in the Institute of Southeast Asian Studies (ISEAS), Singapore (2001–2007), Head of the Centre for American Studies (KAMERA) in the Institute of Occidental Studies (IKON) in the National University of Malaysia (UKM) from 2008 to 2011, and Director of the Institute of Malaysian and International Studies (IKMAS) in UKM from 2011 to 2013. His numerous publications focus on international relations of Southeast Asia, strategic studies, and also ethnic studies. His most recent publication is an edited work titled *Managing Ethnic and Religious Diversity in the United States and Malaysia: Issues, Challenges and Prospects*, jointly published by UKM and USM (Universiti Sains Malaysia) in 2022.

Sivapalan Selvadurai, Ph.D., is an Associate Professor and part-time lecturer attached with the Center of Shaping Advanced and Professional Education

(UKMShape). He is currently a Visiting Associate Professor with the School of Liberal Arts and Sciences, Faculty of Social Sciences and Leisure Management, Taylor's University, Subang Jaya, Selangor, Malaysia. He was formerly attached with the Centre for Research in Development, Social and Environment (SEEDS), Faculty of Social Science and Humanities, Universiti Kebangsaan Malaysia (UKM), Bangi, Selangor, Malaysia. His research interest entails local development issues relating to community development, gender and entrepreneurial development. He has published articles in reviewed journals, including numerous articles in WOS, SCOPUS and ERA indexed journals. He was also the former Head of Research Cluster on Governance and Institution, and Head of Development Science Program under the SEEDS Centre.

Benny Thomas Vivian, Ph.D., is a Senior Lecturer at the Faculty of Social Science and Humanities, Tunku Abdul Rahman University of Management and Technology (TAR UMT). He obtained his Ph.D. in the field of Science Development from National University of Malaysia. His research is mainly focused on religious intolerance, conflict, tension and co-existence. He was a member of Faculty Research and Development Committee in the field of social sciences and humanities. He is currently course coordinator for Ethnic Relations and Malaysian Studies.

www.ingramcontent.com/pod-product-compliance
Lightning Source LLC
Chambersburg PA
CBHW062041270326
41929CB00014B/2502